THE 21ST CENTURY STOCKBROKER: A NEW WAVE

Other books by Daniel C. Montano

How to Manage an Enterprise in Crisis: A Practical
Guide on How to Turn Around an Enterprise from
Crisis Back to Normality.

ISBN 1-883020-01-8

THE 21ST CENTURY STOCKBROKER:
A NEW WAVE

The Catalyst of the World's Economic
and Financial Revolution of the 21st Century

How You Can Become a Stockbroker
And
Why You Should

by
Daniel C. Montano

MONTANO PUBLISHING COMPANY

For information about permission to reproduce selections from this book, write to:

> Permissions
> Montano Securities Corporation
> 500 South Main Street
> Suite 1123
> Orange, CA 92668

Library of Congress Cataloging in Publication Data

Montano, Daniel C.
   The 21st Century Stockbroker: A New Wave

Financial Services Business Book

ISBN 1-883020-00-X

Printed in the United States of America

TGG.XM.II.XX.IXIII

DEDICATION

This book is dedicated to all the dreamers who become doers and are making the world a better place.

Thank you to those people who made this book possible: my chief editor, Lynne Paynter Bolduc; my family; and my partners, especially Mark A. Voorhis, Sammy W. Cross, Judy S. Pelton, Donald W. Clear, Alex G. Montano, and Thomas L. Ingram.

TABLE OF CONTENTS

INTRODUCTION

Welcome to my book, <u>The 21st Century Stockbroker -
A New Wave.</u>

This book has been written to look into the future of the
stockbrokerage business and its affects upon both the Financial Services
Industry and the economy of the world. The convergence of major
trends, such as the aging of the Baby Boomer population, the
Communications and Information Revolutions, and the reblossoming
of the world's economies after the fall of Communism, Socialism, and
other faulty economic programs, is going to revolutionize the world of
finance and the world's economy. The lifestyle changes occurring
throughout the world, both by choice and by competition, will affect
the stockbrokerage business and commerce dramatically over the next
30 years. All of these factors and more are converging into a powerful
force that is going to change the world forever. The catalyst of all of
this financial and economic change will be the stockbroker. Not the
stockbroker of today, but the 21st Century Stockbroker.

The 21st Century Stockbroker will be very different than what
we think of as a stockbroker today. The primary purpose of writing
this book is to share with the reader what I envision those changes to
be and their affects upon commerce and you, now and into the next
30 years.

I have been in the securities business for 25 years. I have been President and Chief Executive Officer of a stockbrokerage firm with over 1300 stockbrokers and I know the stockbrokerage business. Yet, what excites me most about the future of the stockbrokerage business is that I see several new dynamic niches developing for the stockbrokerage business. Fifteen years ago, the discount stockbrokerage business was a new niche in the industry. Many of us within the stockbrokerage business now wish that we had jumped into that new area of the business then, like Charles Schwab did. The developments occurring today are similar business opportunities for the stockbrokerage business. The Part-Time Stockbroker, the Ethnic Stockbroker, and the Internationalization of Capital Markets are just a few of the new niches in the marketplace that I see developing now.

You will find that I tend to start every subject in this book very simplistically and then build up to more sophisticated discussions. This comes from my years as an university professor. Be patient with my wanderings, they will reach a relevant conclusion.

The purpose of this book is to share with you the greatest business in the world and to invite you to participate and profit as a 21st Century Stockbroker. You can become a stockbroker, it is the greatest business in the world, and you can succeed.

August of 1993 will mark the conclusion of my 25th year in the stockbrokerage business. In 1968, when I started on the floor of the Pacific Coast Stock Exchange, little did I realize the wonders that I would see and experience in the stockbrokerage business over the next 25 years. There is no doubt that the securities business is the greatest business in the world. It is financially rewarding, exciting, and dynamic. I believe this high paying, challenging, and dynamic business is the catalyst of every major economic and cultural change in the world today and for the next 30 years.

My purpose in writing this book is, as I now approach the 45th year of my life, I am facing the realization that the last 25 years have passed very quickly. In the 25 years that I have been in the securities business, I have seen the birth of the computer industry and its resulting revolutionary effects upon our society, I have participated in the Communications Revolution, the Medical Science Revolution, and much, much more. In many cases, I have helped finance hundreds of companies in these dynamic new industries. I have financed these companies in their start-up phases and development phases, I have financed them in their growth and expansion phases, and I have financed their financial reorganizations, recovery, and return to prosperity. The securities business has been very good to me. I have been very fortunate over the past 25 years to have been associated with some very brilliant people, people who helped enlighten me as to the future of commerce resulting from the dramatic changes occurring in our society and the world. Throughout my life, I have always loved history with a passion. This is because I believe history teaches us the lessons and secrets of what the future holds for all of us today.

For these reasons, I decided to write this book about the stockbrokerage business of the future, the 21st Century Stockbrokers and their position as the New Wave in our society and the world. This book is my attempt to place into words my vision for the future of the economic and financial world for the next 30 years and to share my vision with anyone who cares to read my analysis of the trends and their resulting effects upon finance. There are several huge massive forces of irresistible changes that are moving though our society with unstoppable force. These massive changes are going to create a New Wave of finance that will revolutionize commerce, culture, and economics over the next 30 years in ways that can only be called "revolutionary."

It is the evaluation of these massive technological and social trends and their converging which I want to share with the reader. Everywhere, the proof of these developments are obvious. The signs and signals of these changes are evident to anyone willing to look. What the effect of these trends is going to be upon our commercial society over the next 30 years are, of course, my personal speculation. When I analyze the irresistible forces that are obvious to me, I see that those forces are going to create the greatest economic miracle ever. The forces creating this New Wave of finance are all occurring now! Business opportunities to profit and prosper over the next 30 years will result from this New Wave of finance.

I believe this New Wave of finance will greatly affect the stockbrokerage business. Not the stockbrokerage business of the 1950's of big offices and centralized execution, not the club of sons of the rich, but the stockbrokerage business of the 21st Century. A business utilizing Star Trek technology and lifestyle, a business of intense competition and tremendous diffusion, a business with hundreds of nationalities and languages. The stockbrokerage business will be the catalyst of an economic and cultural revolution into the 21st Century and beyond. The purpose of this book is to inform as many people, of all ages, all races, all backgrounds that they too can participate and profit in this New Wave of finance and this forthcoming economic revolution <u>as a stockbroker</u>!

Yes, I believe you can become a stockbroker for the 21st Century, even if you are now retired, speak only a foreign language, or are physically handicapped. This is part of the vision I see that is the greatest business opportunity for all people ever. A personal opportunity for you to participate in and profit from the greatest economic wave in the history of mankind. You can participate and profit in this great financial New Wave as a stockbroker. A major part of this book is to open the eyes of the average reader to the fact that it is possible to be a stockbroker and profit from the technological and cultural changes occurring now which are going to democratize finance. Personal, business, corporate, and government finances are going to be available to the average person in ways never before perceived. Age, race, and nationality will cease being disadvantages in finance and instead become advantages. You will see that stockbrokers in the 21st Century will be very different than those of 1950.

Before I go too far into the main topic of this book, let me introduce myself. My name is Daniel C. Montano. I was born in July, 1948, in East Los Angeles as the second son of an Irish-German-American mother who had been raised in North Carolina, and a Mexican-American father who was born and raised in southern California. We were so poor when I was a child that I can easily remember going to bed hungry many times. My parents worked hard, studied, sacrificed, started several small business, and saved and invested for our futures. They taught my brother and I that hard work was a blessing from God and we were each responsible for our own destiny.

I started working my first job when I was 4 years old in our family laundromat, where we washed other people's clothes and fixed the washing machines that seemed to break down every day. From that beginning, I have also worked as a box boy, bus boy, clerk, general laborer, construction worker, painter, cashier, warehouseman, mover, fry cook, dishwasher, plumber, door-to-door salesman, store clerk, field hand and crop picker, street vendor, and more before I was 19 years old.

When I was 19, I was working at Douglas Aircraft in Long Beach, California on the swing shift (4:00 p.m. until midnight). While I was working there, I attended Fullerton Jr. College. I completed my Associates of Arts Degree in 1968. Then I registered at California State University at Los Angeles for my upper division classes.

In August, 1968, realizing that time was racing by me, I felt I had to start in the stockbrokerage business before I lost my youth. I went down to Spring Street in downtown Los Angeles (which was then the Financial District of southern California) and started going door-to-door of stockbrokerage firms asking for a job. No one was interested in hiring me. I was too young (I had just turned 20), I had not completed my education, I was the wrong nationality, and my parents did not have money. Finally, I ended up at the offices of Noble, Cooke & Company where I agreed to start working without pay to prove they should hire me. In the years that followed, I worked on the floor of the stock exchange, on the institutional desk, in the syndicate department, back office, trading desk, and the corporate finance department as I worked my way up through almost every position in the securities industry.

While working full-time, I obtained my Bachelors of Science Degree from California State University at Los Angeles in Business with an emphasis in Accounting. I then received my Masters of Business Administration Degree from the University of Southern California with an emphasis in Finance. Following obtaining my MBA, I became a teacher at Pepperdine University and California State University at Fullerton in their graduate and undergraduate programs. For 7 years, I taught business, accounting, finance, and economics to hundreds of college students. And I did all of this while working full-time at various firms in the stockbrokerage business!

In February, 1979, I started my own securities firm, Montano Securities Corporation. By this time, I had helped manage over 100 new public stock issues for all types of companies from high technology to medical to retail to manufacturing to banking and more. I was now well qualified to run my own successful securities firm.

During the last 25 years, I have served on the Board of Directors of 26 publicly traded companies. I have worked in 48 countries as a consultant to Governments, an advisor to their industries' managers, a lecturer and teacher to these Governments on direct inward investment, business management, and capital markets.

Also during these last 25 years, I have been the Chief Executive Officer responsible for handling the crisis management of 15 enterprises. I have been successful in turning around 14 of the 15 companies. One of those companies was Knudson Dairies, based in Los Angeles, California which then had 1.4 billion dollars in annual revenues. I have also been the Chairman of the Board of a $400,000,000 asset bank.

Besides this book, The 21st Century Stockbroker - A New Wave, I have written a book entitled: How to Manage an Enterprise in Crisis; A Practical Guide on How to Turn Around an Enterprise from Crisis Back to Normality. Additionally, I have written several articles on Capital Markets Development and Business Management and

Development. I have given seminars on capital markets and their development in London, Paris, Amsterdam, Tokyo, Hong Kong, New Delhi, Bombay, Manila, and numerous other major cities.

For the last 25 years, I have been married to Vicki, my high school sweetheart, and we have 4 children, all of whom are grown up and working in the securities business with me at Montano Securities Corporation. My wife and I also have 3 grandchildren so far.

So that is a quick background on myself and my qualifications to write this book. I have been in the securities business for 25 years in every capacity and I have participated in and seen many of the dynamic changes that have already taken place in the securities business.

From what I have seen, the greatest business opportunities for the stockbrokerage business are still out there in the future. I am, by no means, a professional writer, however, these exciting new changes in the Financial Services Industry have compelled me to write this book to share these ideas and business opportunities with those that wish to learn about and participate in the greatest business in the world – the Stockbrokerage Business.

1

THE NEW WAVE TRENDS

The primary subject matter of this book is the major trends that are causing this New Wave in finance and the world's economics. It is important that I explain to the reader what caused me to see these trends and to have these revelations about the future of the securities business. This will help explain why I am so excited about the future of the securities business.

Since 1989, we, at Montano Securities Corporation, have been attempting to develop business in the former Communist countries of Europe and Africa. We have traveled regularly to these countries in attempts to teach them the new world of Capitalism. These trips were always unique events.

In 1991, we hosted several delegations from the former Soviet bloc to southern California. Our purpose was to show them our world and to introduce them to the concepts of a Free Market Economic System and how to do business in that economic and commercial system. Of all the delegations we hosted, the most important was a group that we had visiting from what was then the USSR in June, 1991. We had scheduled a series of high level business meetings for the Soviet delegates. These included visits for them to see many companies in California from high tech electronics, medical, home building, food processing, etc.

The Soviets' visit also coincided with a speech that I was scheduled to give for a business association from the University of Southern California (USC) on "Business Leadership in the 21st Century." We arranged to have the Soviets invited to that meeting so they could hear me speak on this subject. I thought I would be able to impress them with my knowledge and visions of business leadership into the future of the 21st Century.

Well, the week with the Soviets in southern California was unique. They were most excited about common supermarkets because they had food in them. They were excited by a discount swap meet because there were so many goods for sale. These people could not, despite all of our efforts, comprehend the basic principals of Free Market Economics and how to do business. The week with the Soviets grew more and more frustrating as we realized their lack of ability to comprehend the issues of Free Market Economics and how to do business; issues which are so important to us.

The night before my speech to the business association from USC, we organized a cocktail party at my home for our Soviet guests. About 300 people came to meet them and exchange business ideas. The only condition that I placed upon the evening was that, at 9:00 p.m., Star Trek - The Next Generation would be on television and, party or not, I do not miss Star Trek - The Next Generation. At 9:00 p.m. that evening, I dragged the Soviets into my family room to watch Star Trek - The Next Generation. I felt that since they had never seen the greatest show ever made (in my opinion), it would open up their minds to the future of the world. After 10 minutes of watching the program, the Soviets were so obviously disinterested that I felt violated - violated because they could not comprehend and appreciate the concepts of the potentials for the future contained in the program.

The next morning, at my scheduled appearance before the USC group, I threw away my written speech. The events of the night before had caused me to realize certain revelations about myself and the 21st Century, the topic of my speech. The lessons I learned the evening before from my Soviet guests invoked me to ask the audience, "How many people in this room believe there are extraterrestrials in outer space?" About half of the audience raised their hands. I asked, "How many in the room think that their grandchildren will travel into outer space?" Again, about half of the people in the room raised their hands. Then I asked, "How many people think that modern science will cure cancer in your lifetime?" Now, most of those in the room raised their hands. I continued, "How many people in the room respect Klingon traditions?" Only less than a quarter of those present raised their hands.

I then started my speech by saying that we in California are so different from the people in the rest of the world. We easily forget that Russians today are worried about such basics as food, shelter, basic medicine and health care; that 75% of the hospitals in Russia do not have hot water; that food in Russia is in shortage and there may be starvation this winter; and communication is nearly impossible as the telephones in Russia are few and those that exist, seldom work. I explained that we, the majority of citizens in the United States, have left behind the normal tribulations of human bonds and the struggles of the average human's daily life when most of the average citizens in the rest of the world are attempting to obtain food and shelter. Most of us in the United States today are no longer dealing with basic survival issues of life and have moved on to the "Star Trek Economic Revolution."

Ponder this for a moment: The Agricultural Revolution occurred in the 16th and 17th Centuries. This Revolution allowed people to grow more food than they could consume. This provided surpluses of food that resulted in freeing some people in society to have more time to dedicate to personal creativity. That additional human creativity led to the inventions that created the Industrial Revolution. The Industrial Revolution created still more surplus for the society in industry, thus freeing more people for further creative research and scientific endeavors. Those creative endeavors led to the Computer Revolution. Then the Computer Revolution again dramatically increased the productivity of people and therefore the societies, thereby creating even greater human surpluses. This additional surplus freed up still more resources for the creation of the Communications Revolution. The combination of all these commercial revolutions has led to the Medical and Health Revolution which, in turn, has expanded our life expectancy and our quality of life. Every year our quality of life has increased steadily, thereby creating even greater surpluses of knowledge, wisdom, experience, and human creativity.

At the start of the 1900's, life expectancy for a male in the United States was only 45 years. Now, it is approaching 80 years of age. Imagine all the additional opportunities to create and discover and learn that a person has today with that extra 35 years of life. Recognize how little time people had only 90 years ago, they died so young and had so little to work with. Today, computers, telephones, faxes, television, radio, jet travel, and more allow each person to interact and contribute dramatically more personal creativity than any generation in the world has ever dared dream of doing.

So in my speech that morning before the USC business group, I told them that I see the next commercial and cultural revolution for our society as "The Star Trek Revolution." A commercial and cultural revolution in our society where food, shelter, clothing, and basic health care are a given. Today, in the United States, many of us can envision standing next to our food synthesizer and asking it for whatever we wish and it is there for us. Many of us have left behind the concerns of basic survival of life and are now dealing with the more enlightening issues of living.

Look at my generation of Americans, the Baby Boomers. We take food to eat as a given, there is no real hunger or starvation in our generation. In fact, we are the first generation in the history of the human race that seeks out ways <u>not</u> to eat, we diet. Few cave men ever dealt with the concept of dieting. We, the Baby Boomers, are not worried about shelter, we are worried about how <u>big</u> a house we have, not if we have one. Medical care? We Baby Boomers believe that health care is a <u>right</u>, not a luxury.

The next generation of Americans born behind the Baby Boomers are now called by many the Baby Bust Generation. I strongly disagree with this label for my children's generation. They are the first generation of people in the history of humanity which has never been deprived of any of the basics of life. Their challenges have never been how to find food or shelter, but how to "explore new frontiers and go where no man has ever gone before." My children's generation was raised with computers. Today, 17 year olds are as comfortable with computers as my generation was with cars. Their entire perspective of life is one of adventure and discovery. They have no perception of depravation or survival; the basics of life, food, shelter, clothing, and health are a given to this generation. All that is left for this generation is the new frontiers of life's adventures. These children and young adults have the ability to produce and create wonders such as no generation ever before has had. That is the reason that I refer to this generation as the "Star Trek Generation." They were raised on Star Trek and they believe that the lifestyle shown on Star Trek is how people can live. They are creating new worlds of opportunities for mankind because they have such a different perspective of life.

As we look into the future and ask, "Where are we, as a society, going and who will lead us there?", we must study the extension of trends. The trends established by the Baby Boomers extended for 30 years. The trends being established today by the Star Trek Generation will also last for the next 30 years or more. With this enlightened perspective, we can start to extrapolate out the future trends and direction. We can speculate intelligently about tomorrow when we see the direction in which we are truly headed.

Today, the tools of communications, computers, telephones, faxes, and more are all accelerating the rapid decentralization of human relationships and personal contact. This phenomenon is greatly extending and changing our basic concepts of technology in today's and tomorrow's world of commerce. This realization suddenly dawned on me during my speech at USC.

As I proceeded delivering my impromptu speech on Business Leadership in the 21st Century, I realized that I was openly brainstorming with the audience. Brainstorming that revealed to me that we, in America, are accelerating away from the rest of the world in our abilities to create wealth and, more important, to comprehend tomorrow. The rest of the world must still deal with so many traditional problems, problems of food, shelter, clothing, and basic health care. Leaders of these nations must spend so much of their time and energy on saving the industries of yesteryear's Industrial Revolution. The manufacturing of automobiles, the coal industry, steel, and labor are all concepts of yesterday and outdated concepts in the Star Trek future that I foresee our economy moving towards.

I faced the realization that the United States is not only accelerating away from our foreign nation competitors who are still defending the labor movement of the Industrial Revolution of yesterday, but even more importantly, we within the United States are accelerating away from the concepts of the static traditional industries. Those business leaders who are not yet adjusting themselves to the concepts of a "Star Trek Economic Revolution" in their perception of the changes occurring in commerce will fail in the future.

As I completed my speech that morning, I realized that in my 25 years in the securities business, I had been carried along by the currents of these strong and fast moving rivers of social and commercial change without realizing it. The Communications, Computer, Health, and Information Revolutions happening all around me, had started the process of the Star Trekking of America and its commerce. The perception of life and commerce in a Star Trek mindset and its affects upon the future only then stood out before me.

It was only when I had attempted to connect the mindset of my guests from the Soviet Union, which was essentially concerned with basic survival – food, shelter, health, etc., through to the mindset of a person in the 21st Century, where we in the United States are now preparing to compete, did I see the river of technological and cultural changes and the path it has taken, carrying all of us along. The path of this powerful cultural and technological river became clearer to me as I realized where it had already traveled and in what direction it was heading. I then saw where we were all moving towards.

The changes that I see over the next 30 years are going to be dramatic and forceful. Many of those important changes are going to have their greatest commercial affects and impact upon the Financial Services Industry. The resulting changes in commerce and lifestyle will result in what can only be defined as a revolution in the Financial Services Industry. Given the revelations about the future of commerce and finance which I saw on the day of my speech, I decided to write this book and place my thoughts down in writing for those who wish to read my ideas and see the direction I envision for commerce and finance into the 21st Century, and especially the affects of these changes on the stockbrokerage business now and into the future.

The changes I foresee and the resulting revolution within the Financial Services Industry are going to be one of the greatest areas of upheaval during the next 30 years. Most banking, savings institutions, and insurance companies have become static in these rapidly changing times. They have become trapped into second guessing themselves by their present day problems of solving yesterday's bad loans. These Financial Services Industry competitors are trapped in a static commercial situation. Meanwhile, they are under constant and relentless assault from new competitors in the Financial Services Industry utilizing a "Star Trek Mentality."

The primary aggressive competitor that is winning the business is the stockbrokerage firms. These stockbrokerage firms are winning market shares every day from the financial service companies still defending themselves against the problems and concerns of yesterday's Industrial Revolution. Even more damaging to the future of these slumbering giants of the Financial Services Industry is that they are regulated by laws and officials with their minds set in the problems of the 1930's Depression era. While banks are struggling to comfort reactionary bank examiners who are enforcing 1930's banking regulations, the stockbrokers are accelerating the implementation of their business programs to steal away with the commercial banks' customers forever.

The reader should understand that this book is going to address the Financial Services Industry marketplace today and into the future for 30 years. The objective is to understand the affects of these changes upon banks, savings institutions, insurance companies, and others. From my analysis, the stockbrokerage firms are going to become the dominant competitors in the Financial Services Industry.

Let's go over some brief examples for you, the reader, to contemplate concerning the rapid changes occurring within the Financial Services Business at the present time:

Banks are supposed to be in the business of taking deposits from their customers and then loaning those funds to borrowers who want to use those funds. The borrower promises to repay the bank, both principal and interest, for the use of the money. Because of this critical position in the world of commerce, the accumulation and allocation of financial capital, most Governments stepped in to regulate banking in the 1930's. At that time, politicians deemed that banking was too important to the commerce of a society to be left to independent bankers. Governments decided that they had to protect society from the bankers. That was the logic for government intervention and regulation of banking.

The 1930's banking regulations were written by the greatest political minds of that time. Yet, no one could then foresee the invention and effects of the computer, cellular phones, faxes, television, and the possibility that the average person would be living to be 90 years old. So today's regulation of the banks is antiquated at best. In today's world of commerce, most automobile companies loan more money for car loans than banks do! Ford Motor Company's credit subsidiary has billions of dollars of real estate loans in its portfolio. Yes, your home mortgage may be held by Ford Motor Company or General Electric or some unregulated pension fund in Holland. Car loans, home mortgages, credit cards, equipment leases, and more are now issued by many non-bank banks. AT&T Credit Cards, Merrill Lynch Money Market Accounts (with check writing privileges), and Mutual Funds that take deposits and make loans are all some examples of non-bank banks.

The 21st Century stockbrokerage business is the catalyst of commercial change occurring in the United States today and tomorrow. I feel sorry for today's Commercial Bankers in the United States. While they are under vicious competitive assault from modern non-bank banks, their ability to respond to this competition is restricted by Government regulators attempting to implement the 1930's

Industrial Revolution and Great Depression concepts upon banks that must compete in a rapidly changing "Star Trek Economy."

Today, someone in San Diego, California can be solicited by a stockbroker in Dallas, Texas to place their money at Fidelity Group in Boston, Massachusetts. In seconds, via electronic funds transfer, Fidelity (a non-bank bank) can obtain deposits from someone in San Diego. Then Fidelity can turn around and lend that money to a company in Ohio. Fidelity acts like a bank, but is not regulated like a bank. This is a small example of the start of the Financial Revolution occurring now from the new Star Trek Mentality of commerce.

As our society in the United States leaves behind the precepts of the Industrial Revolution and we move into the real commercial effects and benefits of a "Star Trek Economy," you are going to see changes in the Financial Services Industry inconceivable only 20 years ago in the United States. Who will be the catalyst of all of this change and be responsible for this revolution in the Financial Services Industry into the 21st Century? It will be the United State's Stockbrokerage Industry - A New Wave.

Yes, the greatest business in the world today is the stockbrokerage business. Not only is it a high paying, profitable, and prestigious business, it is the catalyst to the coming Economic and Financial Revolution of the 21st Century. When you look at the financial markets today, stockbrokerage firms are scrutinizing mortgage loans, car loans, credit card receivables, student loans, small business loans, equipment financing, and even accounts receivable financing for companies. Stockbrokerage firms are at the vanguard of the Financial Services Revolution that is occurring domestically within the United States and internationally.

The stockbrokerage business is the catalyst of the introduction of the "Star Trek Economic Revolution." This is because it is the stockbrokerage business that rewards creativity. It is the stockbrokerage business where fortunes can be earned by identifying a small change, a small crack of opportunity in the world of finance, commerce, or our culture and society. It is the stockbrokerage business that strives on creating tomorrow today. The stockbrokerage business is dedicated to very personalized service for those with capital or who are in need of capital.

This book is about the greatest business in the world, The 21st Century Stockbroker. It is about the revolutionary changes that are occurring in the world today and tomorrow and how you can participate in these changes.

A personal goal for my stockbrokerage firm is, by the year 2001, to have a women (age 98) on a cruise ship in the middle of the Indian Ocean being a Montano Securities stockbroker. For this woman, while on her cruise ship, to be able to service 20 other retired ladies as her investment clients from 10 different states on a very personalized and professional basis, taking care of their special needs via the Star Trek commercial systems that we and others will be implementing. I want a Montano Securities stockbroker in Srinagar, Kashmir, India who is 31 years old and servicing local investors and businesses out of his home via a laptop computer hooked up to our Corporate Office in Orange, California via a global satellite link. I want a 65 year old retired electronics executive from Ohio to be a part-time Montano Securities stockbroker serving his clients' special investment needs from the 14th tee at his golf club as efficiently as any other stockbroker in the world.

This book is about the greatest business in the world, the stockbrokerage business. This book is about the changes occurring in the cultural and commercial society that we all live within. This book describes the United States' domestic trends and extrapolates them out into the future 30 years. This book will analyze the international financial markets and how they will develop over the next 30 years. Most important, this book will explore how you, the reader, can participate in this massive business opportunity. Yes, you can become a stockbroker and participate in the greatest business opportunity in the world. You can participate as a stockbroker in the 21st Century because it is open to all, regardless of your race, religion, or education. It is a dynamic, exciting, and rewarding business. It is also passionately emotional.

This book is written to share with you my vision of the future of commerce and the stockbrokerage business into the 21st Century. It is written to show how you can participate in this business. If you agree with what you read, you might want to become a stockbroker with us and move into the next frontier of finance, culture, and commerce in the "Star Trek Economy" of the 21st Century. This is an opportunity to enjoy life's adventure and financial security as a stockbroker into the 21st Century.

Thank you for your interest in my ideas and visions about the future of the stockbrokerage business into the 21st Century.

2

WHAT IS A STOCKBROKER ?

What is a stockbroker? This may seem to many readers to be a simple question, yet it is not. Most people's idea of what a stockbroker is are the results of watching television or seeing a movie. Stockbrokers are much more than what is seen in the movies. Stockbrokers are the entrepreneurs that are the heart and soul of the Free Market Economic System. What would the economic system known as Capitalism be without Capitalists and the people that service those Capitalists - the stockbrokers?

For this book to have any meaning to the reader, it is imperative that time be spent on providing the reader with a brief introduction as to what a stockbroker is and what the stockbroker does. This chapter will cover the basic economic role that stockbrokers perform in our economic system today and where I see that role evolving over the next 30 years. To explain the function that stockbrokers perform in our economic society, we must first have a basic economic history lesson. A brief economic history lesson will help explain the importance of stockbrokers in an economic and historical perspective. Then we will be able to build upon that foundation of knowledge to study the business opportunities of the future in the stockbrokerage business.

In the 1700's, Adam Smith attempted to explain in a rational and logical method how free people conduct themselves in consensual commerce. With his writing, The Wealth for Nations, Adam Smith created what is now the Science of Economics. Adam Smith was not attempting to advocate any philosophical position. Mr. Smith was simply attempting to apply rational logic to the commercial conduct of humans and to explain how people conduct themselves in making decisions and the resulting effects upon society. The basic conclusion of Adam Smith was that people who were free to pursue their own interests create greater wealth for everyone within society. These concepts of Free Market Economics that Mr. Smith clarified have been challenged by many others since they were written in the 1700's. Never were the concepts of Free Market Economics challenged more than in the last 90 years. The economic concepts of Communism, Socialism, State Control, The Guiding Hand, Central Planning, and more have all been imposed upon people around the world.

In 1979, approximately 80% of the world's population was under some form of government that denied its citizens the rights to freely commerce within their own societies. After 70 years of social experimentation in economics, those concepts of economics have all <u>failed</u>! Unquestionably, Free Market Economics has demonstrated that it allows people to generate more wealth for themselves and their society than any other form of economics. Why this short economics lesson is important to the future of the 21st Century Stockbroker is that the cliche that is most often used to describe Free Market Economics is the term "Capitalism." Adam Smith stated that there were four major components to Free Market Economics: land, labor, entrepreneurship, and capital. Of these, capital has proven to be the most important and controlling element.

Why are Free Market Economics generally referred to as Capitalism? It is because capital has proven itself to be the most important of the four components of economics. History has proven beyond a shadow of a doubt that those who control capital are the power and control behind the Free Market Economic System. Due to that history, Free Market Economics has also become known as the Capitalism System.

This is why stockbrokers are so important in our society. Stockbrokers are the people that control the life blood of the Free Market Economic System: capital! Stockbrokers accumulate, gather, and then allocate capital. This service function of handling and controlling capital is what a stockbrokerage business is all about.

Wall Street is the location where the highest concentration of stockbrokers exists. Wall Street has become synonymous with the stockbrokerage business. The phrase "Wall Street" is often used to describe the location of the heart of the capital markets. However, the phrase Wall Street is never used to describe the weak and poor in our society; it is a phrase used to describe the rich and powerful. Stockbrokers are the power elite of a Free Market Capitalistic System. The reason is simple: Stockbrokers handle and control the life blood of the Capitalism system – capital.

The power and importance of stockbrokers to the Capitalistic system are reflected by the fact that being a stockbroker is one of the highest paying careers in the world. I recently read that the average income for a stockbroker in the United States is 100% higher than the average income for a lawyer. That's right, the average stockbroker makes twice as much as the average lawyer in the United States! Obviously, being a stockbroker is a high paying and highly prestigious career. The United States Securities Industry Association reported that, in 1992, the earnings for a stockbroker averaged over $114,000 a year. Stockbrokers are one of the highest paid professions in the United States. Their high pay is due to the importance of capital markets in the operations of the Free Market Economic System, also known as Capitalism.

What is the stockbrokers' function in the Free Market Economic system that makes them so important and so well paid? Their function is to act as an intermediary between those who have surplus capital funds and those who want capital. The basic concept that a stockbroker is a financial intermediary will be critical for you to understand what this book is attempting to show you. To understand the effects of the trends that are occurring and creating the 21st Century Stockbroker, you need to keep in mind that stockbrokers are in the industry of financial intermediary. In Chapter Three of this book, I am going to cover the revolutionary changes in the Financial Services Industry in greater detail. That chapter will include all of those competing industries that are in the financial intermediation business such as banks, savings and loans, insurance companies, thrifts, credit unions, pension funds, and more. The primary issue the reader needs to accept here in this chapter is what a stockbroker is. Later in this book, we will compare stockbrokers to their competition in the financial intermediation business.

To summarize a critical point, stockbrokers are in the Financial Services Industry where they provide services as financial intermediaries. Once the reader understands that stockbrokers are in the Financial Services Industry, I can explain historically how they became so powerful and what the future holds for stockbrokers into the 21st Century. Once their economic function is understood, then I can address why stockbrokers are wealthier and more powerful than the others in the Financial Services Business.

To understand the future of stockbrokers in the United States, a brief history lesson is needed. The first step in that history lesson is to understand the stockbrokerage business. The most important step then becomes understanding the laws in the United States that affect stockbrokers and commercial banks.

Several nations, including the United States, have divided the financial commercial functions that were once the business of Merchant Bankers. Merchant Bankers are, or were, in the business of finance that extended from trade and commerce. Basically from early merchants (1400's to 1800's) handling trade and commerce, these merchants eventually developed the business capabilities to handle finance. All of the great financial and banking families of history were Merchant Bankers: Medic, Furger, Rothschild, Baring, Hope, Morgan, etc.

In the United States, the Merchant Bankers grew so wealthy and powerful that they were considered by some to be "Robber Barons." Some writers say that, at the turn of the century in the 1900's, the Merchant Bankers in the United States controlled or owned over 87% of all businesses in the United States. For example, the House of Morgan, owned by J.P. Morgan, was so powerful that several times the United States Government had to turn to Morgan to save the Federal Government from bankruptcy. So powerful were these Merchant Bankers that the United States Government started an investigation into them in the 1910's called the Pujo Committee.

When the Great Depression started after the stock market collapse of 1929, politicians in Washington D.C. turned to and blamed many of the problems of the economy upon the power of these Merchant Bankers. Politicians believed that since it was these Merchant Bankers who controlled capital and commerce throughout the United States, the Merchant Bankers' power had to be restricted. The Presidency of Franklin D. Roosevelt made banking reform one of its primary missions. Out of this political effort, the 1930's legislative reform of banking occurred. One of the primary results was the division of Merchant Banks into two separate parts within the Financial Service Industry. Those two parts are referred to as Commercial Banking and Investment Banking.

A simple description would be that Commercial Bankers were allowed to accept deposits from the general public and to make loans. Commercial Banks could not provide capital for the equity needs of a company or own other businesses, even indirectly. Investment Bankers were allowed to deal in equities, but could not make loans or take deposits. Most Americans think of their local branch of a Commercial Bank as a "bank." Few people think of a stockbroker as a bank and yet that is what a stockbroker is, an <u>Investment Bank</u>.

What has happened in banking over the last 50 years is very simple. Laws put into place by legislators in 1933 to divide the banking powers of Merchant Bankers are now being circumvented by technology and lifestyle. These banking laws were created and established to handle the world as legislators understood it in 1933. No one could then envision the tremendous changes that were to occur in the future of the world. Technology and lifestyle changes would occur that would allow the Investment Bankers to compete freely and return to the economic role of becoming Merchant Bankers again. While stockbrokers are utilizing technology to remake themselves as Merchant Bankers, the 1933 laws have evolved to the point that those laws tie the hands of the Commercial Bankers to compete.

Where Commercial Bankers in the United States have become known for their large buildings and conservative personnel, Investment Bankers are known for their aggressive personnel who only succeed by their wits, creativity, and ability to generate economic results. With the dawning of a new world of technology and commerce, Commercial Bankers are regarded as too conservative or too slow to accept change and as not being risk takers. Investment Bankers are the providers of equity capital for new industries and new methods of commerce. More important, Investment Bankers are forced to compete every day for investor funds and opportunity. Every day, a stockbroker must be competitive to attract sources of capital to fund businesses.

Technological changes in computers and communications have created a very competitive world that can destroy a stockbroker in a very short period of time if the stockbroker does not respond to competitive pressures. Unlike a Commercial Bank that has captive funds held in its savings accounts, stockbrokers are faced with more demanding customers every day. This fierce competition has forced the stockbrokers to become more creative, responsive, and aggressive when it comes to implementing new technology, concepts, and methods of commerce. Equally important, stockbrokers have to watch for any changes in their marketplace or new niches in any marketplace.

This fierce competitive environment has forced stockbrokers to become the agents of change in our economic and commercial society. Look at the facts: Commercial Bankers loan you money based upon last year's financial results. Your tax returns for the past year, your historically accumulated personal collateral, and your past income are all that a Commercial Banker cares about. Commercial Bankers look backwards to analyze what they are going to do financially with a customer. A Commercial Bank's business is to loan you money on the condition that you pay it back with interest. Today's Commercial Bankers do not want to share in the future profits of the venture. Commercial Bankers do not want to hear about what you are going to do in the future, they just want their loan repaid with interest.

Stockbrokers or Investment Bankers are very different: They want to share in the <u>future</u> profits of the business, they want to be part owners in the business, and they want the business to grow and prosper. It was the Investment Bankers who financed the Computer Revolution, the Pharmaceutical Revolution, the Telecommunications Revolution, and every commercial revolution and new development in the world. This passion that Investment Bankers have to seek out new areas of commerce for investment is not derived from some birthright of stockbrokers, but created out of a necessity for their competitive survival.

Once the Investment Bankers have developed a new area of commerce and created an industry, then, and only then, do those industries become <u>bankable</u>. Once a business is proven successful, then the Commercial Banker has historically come along and underpriced the investment returns demanded by a stockbroker's investors. A Commercial Bank's depositors (investors) demanded lower investment returns than a stockbroker's investors historically. Investment Bankers over the last 25 years have been under a self-generated constant competitive pressure to keep pushing new technological horizons, to seek new markets and new areas of commerce by looking into the future.

Stockbrokers are forced by their own competitive pressures to seek out new and creative areas of commerce and business. Stockbrokers have been in the business to finance commercial change because it has become their area of commercial domain. What this has done over the last 50 years in the United States is force the stockbrokers to use the latest technology to compete, compete in any way they can. These new technologies have allowed stockbrokers to transcend the original business domain of Commercial Bankers and to be able to attack the banking business from all sides.

Commercial Banks can only take customer deposits and make loans. Their area of the banking business seems, at first glance, to be safe. Yet today, you can have a checking account at Merrill Lynch, a credit card from Dean Witter, and a mortgage loan from Shearson. The stockbrokers have utilized the tremendous commercial flexibility provided by the Communications Revolution to bypass the intent of laws written in 1933 to limit the banking industry. Stockbrokers have used these technologies to innovate themselves back into being, in reality, Merchant Bankers again. Stockbrokers are now recapturing the financial role historically performed by Merchant Bankers. Their new found strength and power are only now beginning to be developed and implemented. The 21st Century Stockbrokers, from what I foresee in the future of banking and the Financial Services Industry, will be Merchant Bankers again. This evolution is good for America, the world, and all of the citizens of the world.

THE 21ST CENTURY STOCKBROKER - A NEW WAVE OF MERCHANT BANKERS

Merchant Bankers were the great developers of the world: railroads, steel, chemicals, telephones, electricity, shipping, communications, farming, health and medical care were all developed by people that were Merchant Bankers or acted like Merchant Bankers under a different legal name. The world today is a poorer place because politicians accepted the economic lie that social planning was a better way to create wealth for their people. The attempts by most Governments to restrict their Merchant Bankers' role in the development of those nations has delayed the development of their nations by 20 to 70 years. Now, stockbrokers can utilize today's technology to recapture the position of the Merchant Banker and start again developing the world's wealth for the benefit of all.

Stockbrokers are financial firms that are flexible innovators. Stockbrokers in today's world of commerce can identify and attack a market niche quickly and then dominate it. Please understand that I am not saying that Commercial Bankers are not capable of being creative. What I am saying is that:

1. Banking legislation passed in 1933 has hampered the Commercial Bankers from being able to adequately compete with the Investment Bankers' new found commercial powers;

2. That, along with the commercial banking crisis that developed in the 1990's (bad loans to third world countries, real estate loans, leveraged buyout loans, etc.), has forced Commercial Bankers to spend a great deal of time and effort curing yesterday's problems;

3. The loan crisis in the banking industry has happened at the same time as the banking regulators clamped down on Commercial Banks' operations; and

4. These relentless regulatory pressures are forcing Commercial Banks back into the competitive environment of the 1930's.

Commercial Banking regulators are attempting to restrict Commercial Bankers more today than at any other time in the history of banking in the United States. Banking regulators are clamping down when what Commercial Bankers need is to be free to openly compete. The freedom to be able to compete in today's rapidly changing Financial Services Business is not a luxury, but a necessity. As long as Commercial Bankers have their hands tied behind their backs by the banking regulators, the Financial Services Business is going to become the domain of the stockbrokers. I foresee that the regulators will over-regulate the Commercial Bankers for the next 20 years and that is good for stockbrokers for the next 20 years.

Recognize that stockbrokers are agents of change. This is because they are only rewarded when they out-perform the competition. Stockbrokers' investment returns must out-perform those available from other competitors in the Financial Services Business, like Commercial Banks, otherwise the stockbroker is out of business. Stockbrokers must offer those people who have surplus capital greater investment returns for that capital than the Commercial Banks or others in the Financial Services Business. If stockbrokers cannot provide better investment returns for investors, those providers of capital will just leave their money sitting passively at a Commercial Bank to earn low interest.

This competitive reality has forced stockbrokers to look into the future and seek opportunities to finance new and creative industries. Stockbrokers are forced by competitive pressure to seek new ways of doing business within our society and new ways to compete with Commercial Banks and others in the Financial Services Business and, most importantly, to succeed.

What is a stockbroker? Stockbrokers are part of the Financial Services Industry, the part that is directly tied to the concept of being "results related." Stockbrokers are at the forefront of change and innovation in the financial services world and thus, at the forefront of the entire world of commerce. The balance of this book is going to explain a stockbroker and his or her role in the world of commerce and Free Market Economics. This book will explain the stockbroker's role in the commerce of our society both today and tomorrow.

What is very important to remember in reading this book is that stockbrokers in the United States are the leaders of the Capitalist economic system, both in the United States and in the world. There are many industries where the United States claims to be the world's leader: computers, medicine, bio-tech, software, etc. Let me assure you, beyond a shadow of a doubt, in the area of Capitalism, the United States is the unquestioned world leader. Leadership in every area of Capitalism: commercial and business systems, methods, concepts, applications, and technology. What is even more impressive is that the United States stockbrokerage industry holds a technological lead over foreign stockbrokerage industries by decades over the nearest competitor. The United States' leadership in the business of Capitalism is its greatest asset to dominate economic and commercial developments over the next 30 years and well into the 21st Century.

Politicians of many Governments in many nations of the world are giving speeches about their efforts to improve the lives of their citizens. Those attempted efforts to create a wealthier society for their people are almost always directed at attracting new industries into their nations, industries to create employment for their citizens. These politicians continually talk of their efforts to invite foreign companies to transfer their production or services technologies into their nation. To a logically rational person or anyone who has studied economic history, these ideas are humorous. While these foreign nations are inviting outside companies into their countries to stimulate their economies, they are ignoring or handicapping the most important of all the industries in their nation's future: the Financial Services Business. Instead of seeking out steel plants, automobile manufacturing, and electronics companies, what the world's nations should import and develop is the industry of Capitalism, the stockbroker!

Could the United States have such diverse and dynamic new companies, creating new industries and new jobs, if it had no stockbrokers to raise the equity capital to finance those ideas? NO! Would America have Apple Computer, Microsoft, Wal Mart, cellular telephones, medical and bio-tech companies if America did not have a vibrant, healthy, and competitive stockbroker industry? NO! The United States owes much of its economic miracle to the stockbrokers and their business function of raising capital and serving financial needs of new industry. Historically, Merchant Bankers and today, stockbrokers are what has made America economically and commercially great. Stockbrokers in the United States have financed the future of America. They always have and they always will.

Other nations of the world must realize that first you develop the capital markets, then the rest of a nation's development will happen naturally. Nations that do not learn that simple and obvious lesson will remain forever in economic trouble. If you do not develop the capital markets of a nation, you cannot develop the nation, economic, historical, and commercial fact.

As we approach the 21st Century, it is interesting and exciting that the rest of the world's leaders are now rejecting all forms of contaminated commerce by their Governments. Communism, Socialism, and Government Guiding Hand are all being rejected and nations everywhere are now returning to the basic economic principals of Free Market Economics. That trend means all of these nations will now have to learn about the stockbrokerage business. The reason being is that you cannot have a Capitalist economic society without the Capitalist and those businesses that serve the Capitalist: the stockbrokers! This means that the whole world must come to the United States to study our leadership in this critical industry, the stockbrokerage business. In their quest to develop their own nations, every nation must start the development of their investment banking and stockbrokerage businesses if they are going to succeed. The 21st Century Stockbroker is a high growth international business!

What is a stockbroker? A stockbroker will be the most important business and professional career for the next 30 years, everywhere in the world. It is a high paying, prestigious business and career. It is a challenging and dynamic profession with a tremendous future. Most important about the stockbrokerage business is that now, today, it is beginning its greatest growth phase in the history of commerce.

The balance of this book is going to explain the Financial Services Industry and why the stockbrokerage business is such a high growth business with a great future. We will also discuss the stockbrokerage business' internal revolution that I foresee for the business into the 21st Century. The book will include some examples of types of people that I foresee becoming 21st Century Stockbrokers in the future and the procedures required in the United States to become a stockbroker. This book will tell how I believe you, the reader of this book, can develop your personal future as a stockbroker. It will tell you about my concepts of a unique business opportunity for an ethnic securities distribution network throughout the United States and internationally. Last, this book will tell you about my company, Montano Securities, and about why you should consider becoming a stockbroker and how you can go about doing that.

What is a stockbroker then? It's your future!

3

THE FINANCIAL
SERVICES INDUSTRY TODAY

This book is about the "21st Century Stockbroker, A New Wave"-a New Wave for commercial, economic, and social change for the United States and the world. For you, the reader of this book, to truly appreciate the stockbrokerage business now and into the future you need to have a brief background of the entire Financial Services Industry. This will be very basic for the sophisticated reader, but for most readers, my perspective will be different in explaining the Financial Services Industry. In this discussion, the Financial Services Industry includes commercial banks, savings institutions, insurance companies, and stockbrokerage firms.

Remember, the Financial Services Industry is comprised of all of these businesses which act as intermediaries. Financial intermediaries are those who perform a service of acting between those who have excess capital and those who want or need capital. These financial intermediaries offer different services or investment products to accomplish that same commercial function. Fundamentally, the intermediaries are all doing the same thing: gathering money from savers and then providing funds to the wanters of capital. To appreciate the new commercial dynamics occurring within the stockbrokerage business, you must briefly review each of these competitors in the Financial Services Business and their competitive position versus stockbrokers both today and for the next 30 years.

COMMERCIAL BANKS

Banks, as we know them in the United States, are generally Commercial Banks. The business of a Commercial Bank is to gather funds deposited by savers. Banks accomplish this by offering depositors of funds low interest rates for the money they deposit into checking accounts and savings accounts. Commercial Banks then take the deposited funds they have gathered and loan the funds out at a higher rate of interest. Examples of such transactions would be a Commercial Bank making car loans, business loans, mortgages, and credit cards.

The difference between the bank's cost of funds (the interest rate paid to depositors for the money left with the bank) and the interest rates that the bank receives for loaning those funds to borrowers is called the Interest Rate Margins or the Interest Rate Spreads. A simple example: A bank pays interest to its depositors at 3% and then loans the depositors' money to a borrower for a car loan at 10% interest. The difference between the bank's cost of funds (3%) and the interest rate it charges the borrower (10%) is 7%. This 7% is the bank's Interest Rate Margin.

The Interest Rate Margin that the bank generates is used by the bank to:

1. Pay the bank's operating overheads;

2. Build up the financial reserves of the bank for possible bad loans (if any loans are not repaid); and

3. Generate profits for the owners of the bank.

This Interest Rate Margin is a very important concept to keep in mind when studying the Financial Services Business. Most companies in the Financial Services Business earn their primary income based upon Interest Rate Margins, the difference between their cost of funds and the interest they earn from borrowers. The Communications and Information Revolution ahead of us is directly attacking this spread known as the Interest Rate Margin. This area of focus is critical for the reader to envision the future.

Commercial Banks are under tremendous competitive assault by stockbrokers who are taking away Commercial Banks' base business. In 1960, I read that Commercial Banks formerly provided over 85% of all funds borrowed in the United States. Today, I understand that the percentage is down to 28% and dropping.

Why? Because of all the revolutionary changes that are occurring in the Financial Services Business. Changes which are allowing stockbrokers to win the marketplace away from Commercial Banks. I will cover those changes and their effects after I have introduced all of the competitors in the Financial Services Business. Those competitors need to be viewed for a complete prospective of the entire marketplace for the Financial Services Industry.

SAVINGS INSTITUTIONS

Savings Institutions are generally savings and loans, savings banks, credit unions, thrifts, pensions funds, and the like, that basically gather funds from people. Their business has the same basic concept as commercial banking, except here the depositor will agree to leave the funds on deposit for a longer period of time in return for a higher promised investment return. These savers and investors agree to leave their money on deposit for a longer period of time because they are saving money for their future and do not need quick access to those funds. In exchange for that understanding (that the money will be deposited for a longer period of time), the depositors can receive a higher rate of interest on their funds. Example: If the Commercial Bank is paying 3% interest for short term deposits, then the Savings Bank might be paying 4% to a depositor for a longer term.

These Savings Institutions generally reloan the deposited funds out in areas that are anticipated to be longer term loans, such as mortgages. Generally, longer term loans earn a higher rate of interest than short term loans. Savings Institutions also have less administrative cost and ongoing paperwork required for their loans. For example, once the Savings Institution makes a 30 year mortgage loan, it has less ongoing paperwork than a Commercial Bank which every year must reappraise the credit worthiness of a business borrowing for its inventory purchases.

These Savings Institutions have been historically less regulated than the banks. They were semi-deregulated in the early 1980's. This semi-deregulation was the worst of both worlds and everyone is aware of the ongoing Savings and Loan debacle in the United States.

INSURANCE COMPANIES

Insurance Companies are also members of the Financial Services Industry. The Insurance Companies' business is to calculate the statistical odds of an event occurring and then collect sufficient premiums to cover their exposure to the anticipated loss. The gathering of these premium funds are then invested by the Insurance Company to earn an Interest Rate Margin profit while they wait for the events that they insured against to happen.

An example would be life insurance. A life insurance company calculates the statistical odds of a person dying, then sets a certain premium to charge for an insurance policy. The Insurance Company then calculates a rate of investment return needed for those premium funds they have just gathered. The calculation of the premiums include what the Insurance Company must charge to fulfill those commitments to a customer, profitably.

Through the use of a sales force, Insurance Companies basically gather funds and then reloan them. Those funds earn a higher investment return for the Insurance Company than the company committed to their policy holders. That is how Insurance Companies earn a profit.

When you remove the actuarial calculations of early premature death from an Insurance Company, what remains is a company that gathers funds from policy holders and then invests those funds. The Insurance Company obtains a higher investment yield than those investment yields they committed to their policy holders. Very similarly to Commercial Banks and other savings institutions, Insurance Companies gather funds and reloan them with the intent of earning an Interest Rate Margin or Spread.

STOCKBROKERS

Stockbrokers are also members of the Financial Services Industry. Generally however, stockbrokers do not base their primary revenues and profits upon Interest Rate Spreads and Interest Rate Margins. The only exception to that statement is the Interest Rate Spread that stockbrokers earn on their customers' Margin Accounts. This is a major component of a stockbrokerage business, but it is not the basis of the stockbrokerage firm's main commercial function in business as it is in the other arenas of the Financial Services Business.

The major difference between stockbrokers and the other competitors in the Financial Services Industry is that stockbrokers earn a commission from matching providers of capital with wanters of capital. Stockbrokers' efforts are utilized in finding higher investment returns for their investing customers or lower costs of capital for their customers who want capital. Over the years, stockbrokers have learned that they must offer their investors higher investment returns than the other competitors in the Financial Services Industry, such as banks. This causes stockbrokers to seek higher investment yields for their investing customers. In fact, banks, savings institutions, and insurance companies are some of the best <u>customers</u> of stockbrokerage firms.

When the other competitors in the Financial Services Business are seeking higher investment returns for their funds, they basically have two ways to place their investment funds. One is through their own creation of investment products. For example, a bank can make a loan to a depositor for a car loan, thereby creating its own user of funds, and earning the bank a higher rate of investment return. The second way is for those financial services organizations to review investment opportunities offered to them by others. Those others can be all sorts of people, but the most common source is undoubtedly the stockbroker. Yes, banks, savings institutions, and insurance companies all call their stockbrokers to seek out higher paying investments for their depositors' funds. Stockbrokers seek out those who want capital and attempt to match them with those who have capital, and that includes banks, savings institutions, and insurance companies.

The important difference to note is the way that the other financial services competitors do their core business. All of the other competitors in the Financial Services Industry (other than stockbrokers) make their primary operating revenues from the Interest Rate Spread. Stockbrokers earn their primary source of revenues from commissions in placing or dealing in better performing investments. This means that those who want capital and can qualify prefer to obtain their capital needs from stockbrokers directly.

The stock exchange, in general, is a better source of funding for companies than the banks. The basic reason is funds provided from stockbrokers are generally cheaper than the cost of funds from banks. Equally true is that savers of capital prefer dealing with the stock exchange to employ their excess funds. This is because historically, the savers of capital earn higher yields on their investment capital from investing in stocks and bonds than they would from a Commercial Bank.

In simple terms, stockbrokers earn their money by being aggressive middlemen between those who have money and those who want it. As compensation for their efforts, stockbrokers charge a one time fee or commission. That commission fee compares with banks' fees of charging interest to earn themselves an Interest Rate Margin Spread. A simple example: A person deposits $100,000 at a Commercial Bank for a promised investment return of 3% per year on their savings for a 5 year period. The Commercial Bank then reloans that same money to a business to purchase a piece of equipment. The business borrows the money from the Commercial Bank with the promise to repay the loan in 5 years at an annual interest rate of 12%. The Interest Rate Spread the bank is earning is 9% (the difference between the cost of funds for the bank - 3% and the anticipated earnings from the loan to the business - 12%). Both the provider of the capital and the user of the capital are jointly paying the bank for its services as a financial intermediator. The bank is earning an Interest Rate Margin of 9% annually on the money being utilized. That computes out to interest income for the bank of $9,000 per year. For 5 years, that equals $45,000 on $100,000 of capital.

A stockbrokerage firm justifies its fees by eliminating the Interest Rate Spread. Stockbrokers do this by bringing the two parties together directly. Example: If someone has a surplus of funds of $100,000 they could, through a stockbroker, deal directly with the borrower. They could mutually agree to an interest rate of 8% per year for the use of those funds for the same 5 years. That would save the business $3,000 per year in interest costs and pay the saver an additional $5,000 per year. The saver would receive $5,000 more per year than he or she would from the bank. This simple example is to demonstrate that the other competitors in the Financial Services Business earn their money by having sufficient Interest Rate Margin Spreads and stockbrokers earn their money by eliminating those very same Interest Rate Margin Spreads.

Now, some of you readers may be saying, "Wait a minute there, Montano, you keep talking about interest rates and stockbrokers generally deal in stocks, not interest rates." Well, one of the major parts of most stockbrokers' business is bonds, which are just transferable loans. Putting that aside, all stocks must compete against bonds and savings (directly or indirectly) as an alternative earnings method for investment capital. A stockbroker must offer better returns on investments to their clients as compared to bank deposits or the bonds that they trade. All stock investment returns are directly or indirectly compared to the yields a person could have earned on bonds or savings accounts. In the stockbrokerage business, we are always comparing how much the stock market investments earned compared to investments in bonds. Competition between investment products is always present and the real measure is how much the investor will earn compared to the risk.

This brief overview of the Financial Services Business all leads to understanding the Financial Services Industry now, today. This basic understanding of the Financial Services Business will also help the reader understand what I see as the start of the greatest commercial change in the history of finance, which is occurring now. Over the next 30 years, the Financial Services Business is going to change rapidly as the 21st Century Stockbroker proves to become the New Wave of evolution and domination within the Financial Services Business of the world.

4

CHANGES IN THE FINANCIAL SERVICES INDUSTRY - TODAY AND TOMORROW

The Financial Services Industry, like many other industries in the world today, is undergoing many changes. These changes are affecting how business is conducted today and the future of business. The Financial Services Industry is awakening to the dawning of a new competitive world. In this new competitive world, stockbrokers are creating much of the change that is occurring. Stockbrokers are seeking out new niches within the Financial Services Business in which they can apply new technologies and new concepts and thus, expand their business.

Of the many changes occurring within the Financial Services Business, there are seven that will most materially affect the future of finance. This chapter will discuss those seven major changes and their affects upon the Financial Services Industry in general and the stockbroker specifically.

CHANGE ONE: THE RAPID CHANGE OF TECHNOLOGY IN COMMUNICATIONS

When the core laws of the Financial Services Industry were written in 1933 and 1934, they were written by the best legislative minds of that time. However, those people could never have imagined the Communications Revolution that is hitting the world today. In

1933, the primary forms of communication were the mails, messenger, some telephones, and telegrams. The most common method of communication was in person, face-to-face communication. People physically went to the bank because that was the primary method of communication in 1933. Across long distances (then defined as distances of 100 miles or more), telegraph was the preferred method of communication. We must remember that traveling 100 miles in 1933 was more difficult than today. A train trip from New York City to Washington D.C. was an all day trip in 1933.

When the Financial Services Industry laws were written in 1933, no one could foresee the invention of the computer, fax machines, telephones like we have today (such as cellular phones), modems, and jet travel. The concept of computer wire transfers of funds or 24 hour global securities trading could not have been envisioned by the regulators of 1933. The world's Communications Revolution has created an opportunity that is revolutionizing the Financial Services Business. Investors throughout the world can now place their funds anywhere in the world, thereby chasing the best investment yields offered throughout the entire world via the computer and 24 hour trading screens. For instance, if a German company wants to borrow $50,000,000 for a new plant and equipment, it can effectively place its request on a computer hooked up to the computer networking system that advertises the company's desire to borrow funds to everyone in the world. Example: "BMW Company is willing to pay X% for $50,000,000 for 2 years."

Additionally, investors around the world can seek out the highest investment yields in any currency they desire. If Japanese yields are 7% and German yields are 9%, the investors, even in Japan, today can take the higher German yields. A retiree in Florida can search through his personal computer for the highest yields available anywhere in the United States from 300 competing savings institutions via a data base hooked into his personal computer.

A stockbroker today can be playing golf on the 14th green on a resort 700 miles from his office. When his office computer notifies his secretary that a certain stock has now reached a desired selling point, the stockbroker's secretary can link the stockbroker's customer, who is in his car driving to a luncheon meeting, with the stockbroker on the golf course via their cellular phones. They can communicate about their next investment objectives, even though they are 700 miles apart and one of them is traveling at 60 miles per hour. At the conclusion of their telephone call, the stockbroker can inform his secretary to modify the customer's sell orders through their office computers, thereby informing the execution specialist on the floor of the New York Stock Exchange what price the customer will sell his shares. The time involved in this scenario is approximately 3 minutes.

Yes, this is the Communications Revolution that will change the face of finance forever.

CHANGE TWO: THE DECENTRALIZATION OF EVERYTHING

Several futurists have written books looking into the future. The most common thread running through these books is the belief that the future will be almost completely decentralized. How will this affect finance in the 21st Century? Once upon a time, people traveled downtown to see their bankers. Once upon a time, people congregated together to see a movie at a theater. Once upon a time, buyers and sellers of securities mutually met at the floor of the Stock Exchange to trade securities. Now everything is decentralizing. You can bank via your home computer. Banks not only have branches everywhere, but progressive banks now have pick-up and delivery services for the bank's business customers. People can still go to a theater to see a movie or they can watch one on television, cable, or rent a video and watch a movie at home. Soon people will be able to dial up through their home telephone system and access almost every motion picture and documentary ever created.

Stockbrokers and stock exchanges are now finding that their common meeting place (which was a requirement to competitive success only 20 years ago) is now a disadvantage. Computer networking trading systems now offer quicker and more competitive alternatives to stock exchanges.

The entire concept of decentralization permeates more than just what I have described here. It is now the preferred cultural condition of our society. Once upon a time, people moved to the city, they centralized. They did this to benefit from the advantages of concentration. Now the opposite is true, people in the wealthier parts of the world seek solace and commerce in the suburbs away from the congestion of the cities.

Management training used to be about "management pyramids" of hierarchy structures. We used to be taught about centralized management and we then trained others in centralized management systems. Now, everyone is attempting to decentralize management and create individual accountability.

The futurists all believe that decentralization is the wave of the future and I agree with them. You will see this will have a tremendous affect upon the Financial Services Industry for the next 30 years.

CHANGE THREE: FLEXIBILITY

The Telecommunications Revolution and the trends towards decentralization are providing a tremendous amount of flexibility to everyone. Choices that only 20 years ago were unimaginable to a consumer, today are common. Medical doctors in Seattle can consult with a medical specialist in Pittsburgh as they jointly review via high resolution video, a CAT-SCAN of a patient in Houston. Children can be shown videos on subjects that allow them to visualize a topic within minutes; subjects that before would have required weeks of long boring lectures to present and still would not be understood by half of the class, today can be visualized and understood in 30 minutes. Flexibility has allowed Avon to sell cosmetics without department stores and counters to display them. Additionally, the flexibility of jet travel opens up new realities of commercial and personal flexibility. I have left my office at 5:00 p.m. on a Tuesday to fly to London from Los Angeles to have a luncheon meeting to clarify a person's misunderstanding of what my company was proposing. I then flew back the next morning to arrive back in my office on Thursday to implement our project plan. That is flexibility.

The flexibility available today is revolutionizing the way we live and do business. What I see for tomorrow is going to revolutionize the way we live even more. This is especially true of the computer literate, jet setting baby boomer population. Their lifestyle flexibility will be phenomenal and their lifestyle options are growing greater every day. The Baby Boomers may be the first generation in history to be so productive and flexible enough to have their cake and eat it too, as a possible commercial reality. Their children's generation, my Star Trek Generation, will be able to undertake commercial tasks and lifestyle choices due to this cultural flexibility that we today cannot even conceive.

Many great historians, when reflecting upon the events of human culture over recorded history, have always stated that human society seems vibrant between periods of rapid change and periods of stagnation. This can also be restated as between periods of no cultural flexibility and great flexibility. The next 30 years are going to be a period of such great flexibility in the society of the United States that it will make the last 30 years seem like a period of stagnation.

This greater flexibility is already being demonstrated everywhere in the Financial Services Business. The exciting part is that you haven't seen anything yet! Over the next 30 years, the Financial Revolution's flexibility will be so phenomenal that we cannot, even today, speculate on the freedom and opportunity this will provide to the savers of capital and the users of capital.

While flexibility is difficult to quantify and impossible to account for, it is a very major trend and change within our society. You cannot see computer software or touch it, yet it has changed all of our lives and it is just beginning.

CHANGE FOUR: TRUST REASSESSMENT

One of the major causes of the Financial Services Industry Revolution is the reassessment of trust. This reassessment of trust is occurring by both the providers of capital and users of capital. Once upon a time, everyone knew that their bank or local savings and loan was safe and that the Federal Government guaranteed their deposit through Federal Depositors Insurance Corporation (FDIC) meaning 100% safety. The big household Financial Services Industry names were where a customer's savings were always safe. Unfortunately, that trust is all being reassessed now by the investing public. The savings and loans debacle has caused great concerns among savers of capital. The banks, their bad loan problems, and their failures have amplified all of these fears and caused savers to reassess who they can trust with their money.

Most people have little faith in the financial soundness of the Federal Government's Social Security System or in other Government promises that "Big Government" will take care of you. Even household names have lost their trusted reputation as savers have learned harsh lessons. When E.F. Hutton talked, people used to listen. When Lincoln Savings and Loan advised, people used to follow. When Executive Life Insurance sold a policy, people used to feel comforted that their finances were safe. No longer do people give their trust so readily.

This reassessment of trust contemplates more than savers and investors. Workers used to trust their retirement knowing their company's pension plan was going to take care of them when they retired. Now those workers are fighting and suing their former employers to receive what was promised. Now workers worry about what the real financial situation is for their future retirement benefits.

The Financial Services Industry is based upon trust. No industry's future is more directly related to the savers' and investors' need for trust than the Financial Services Industry. The Financial Services Industry asked savers to entrust their excess capital to them to be held safely and return when requested. All of that trust is now being reassessed.

The Financial Services Industry regulations of the 1930's were originally created to return trust to the Financial Services Business during the Great Depression. That trust is now under serious reassessment for the first time since the Great Depression. That process of reassessment of trust will not stop during the next 30 years. Unlike the 1930's when the Federal Government stepped forward to assure savers their money was safe because the Federal Government guaranteed the money, today the Federal Government's guarantee is on everything and people have lost faith in its real value. Investors have seen too many games already played by the Government to relax their concerns again.

The Communications Revolution, the decentralization of financial services, and the flexibility available to savers and investors opens up an ongoing and continual ability to reassess every vendor and provider in the Financial Services Industry. The trust reassessment issue is going to create new competitors in the Financial Services Business as the savers of capital demand different degrees of trust. The trust reassessment occurring in the marketplace today is challenging the old institution's concept of investor trust and offering opportunities to the new providers of the concept of investor trust.

CHANGE FIVE: CHANGES IN THE WANTERS AND USERS OF CAPITAL

Most of the changes covered so far have addressed the savers of capital. Equally true, the revolution in the Financial Services Business will be driven by the users of capital. Whether those users of capital are home buyers, car buyers, equipment purchasers, importers, builders of houses, Venture Capitalists, or Governments, they will be more demanding and more qualified to measure performance than ever before.

The Communications Revolution, decentralization, and greater flexibility have created more opportunities for the users of capital today and in the future. An even more important development is the educational enlightenment of how financial markets work. This has created a very enlightened user of capital.

In the 1950's, the president of a growing manufacturing company was awestruck by the mystical powers on Wall Street and their secret world of finance, a world that he could not grasp the concept of, even if it had been offered. He paid the fees to his investment bankers and left much profit on the table for them because he did not understand.

In 1992, the high tech companies that are going public generally have internal personnel who have personally experienced the process of raising capital many times. Those companies' early stage Venture Capitalists were, or are, Investment Bankers themselves. None of those investment professionals want to leave too much profit on the table for the other Investment Bankers. Those who raise capital ("issuers") know almost as much about the financial markets as the Investment Bankers.

Major companies now have virtually direct access to the short term money markets through commercial paper. Many companies can now access insurance companies directly to obtain their capital needs. The world is changing as the users of capital are becoming more and more sophisticated and experienced. This will also be a major cause of the Financial Services Revolution of the next 30 years.

The mystical world of finance is slowly being revealed to the users of capital and the Information Revolution is enlightening them on how it works and how they can better utilize the capital markets.

CHANGE SIX: THE FINANCIAL REGULATION HANDICAP

One of the major reasons I see for the Financial Services Revolution over the next 30 years is the handicap of regulation that is now being placed upon the Commercial Banks. Commercial Banks are extremely regulated. Their regulation was originally created in the 1930's to monitor the operational prudence of Commercial Banks. This was done so the banks' customers (depositors) would regain their trust in the banking system. The original objective of regulation was that depositors would know the Commercial Banks were being operated prudently and on a sound business basis.

This original regulatory review of operational prudence has gradually expanded to the point where regulators now make qualitative reviews of more than a Commercial Bank's operational procedures and policy. Now, regulators are reviewing and regulating social and political correctness of a bank's operating and policy procedures. Banking regulators are reeling from the financial disaster of the Savings and Loans Crisis, the banks' third world loans, and now from their real estate loan problems. In a standard human reactionary and bureaucratic manner, the regulators are overreacting to the wrong problems in the wrong way.

Even worse, regulators of the Commercial Banks are not held accountable to anyone for their actions and accusations. The regulators are now demoralizing the officers and directors of banks and savings and loans. These bank regulators are looking into and judging bank officers and directors about what actions the institution should have or did undertake. Those decisions by the banks' management and directors are now being second guessed and challenged by the bank regulators. The bank regulators are now making executive, management, and operational directives to the board of directors and management of Commercial Banks.

Regulators are now suing bank and savings and loan directors for what they should have done instead of whether there was any evil intent in what they did. In plain words, if a bank director made a reasonable decision at the time the decision was made, the regulators should not be reviewing them today by a different standard. Example: Three years later, the regulators are saying, "You should not have made these real estate loans to XXX because XXX defaulted." Well, at the time the bank made the real estate loans, they seemed good. The borrower was believed to be a good credit risk and the directors of the bank supported the bank's management recommendation to make the loan. Is this justifiable grounds for suing bank directors? Regulators should not be challenging the banks' decisions years later because loans turned out to be inappropriate and the bank directors should have been better predictors of the future. Although there is no evidence of bad faith, bank directors are being sued by bank regulators for having done a bad job of seeing into the future. If that standard were applied to politicians, they would all be in jail.

The issue I am addressing here is that it only takes one innocent and honest bank director to be sued on an arbitrary basis. Once that happens, some good and capable bank directors will resign to avoid the capricious liability being created by reactionary bank regulators seeking someone to punish. The bank directors remaining at banks are now forced to become extremely defensive.

Remember, today one group of bank regulators are on one hand telling banks they must lend in higher risk areas (no red lining). The banks are being told they must lend where historically there has been greater credit risk and loan losses. Then, another group of bank regulators tells the banks to improve the quality of loans because the bank has too much exposure to loan losses. One group of banking regulators is classifying bank loans, thereby decreasing the ability of the bank to lend, while another group of regulators is pressuring the banks to lend more to troubled borrowers to save the economy. You think you are confused! Be glad you are not a bank director exposed to being sued <u>criminally</u> for not understanding what all of these regulators are demanding.

The regulation of the Financial Services Industry needs to be explored at this point so the reader can understand how this is going to affect the Financial Services Industry in the future. The summation of this regulation can be divided into two parts:

Part One: Those businesses in the Financial Services Industry that tell their providers of investment funds (the depositors) they have little or no risk investing with them. One of the major reasons for that belief is because of the fact that these businesses have some sort of form of Government insurance support assistance. Example: FDIC Insurance.

Part Two: Those businesses in the Financial Services Industry that tell the providers of their funds what the risks are and that the providers must bear the risk.

Banks, savings and loans, insurance companies, pensions, thrifts, etc. attract their funding sources via the promise of no or very little risk of principal or income. They are all under an unparalleled regulator assault. Regulators are attempting to assure the depositors that they have no risk. Thus, banks, savings and loans, insurance companies, pensions, thrifts, and the like fit into group one of the two regulatory groups above.

Securities firms fit into group two and their regulation is very different. Securities firms are held accountable only in that they must disclose the risk to the investor and they are not under a qualitative regulatory assault. This means that while the banking industry is reregulating itself to the inquisition of regulators, the stockbrokerage firms can attack every new market niche in the Financial Services Industry they can identify. The stockbrokers can do this as long as they disclose the risk of the investment to an ever increasingly sophisticated financial marketplace. With an ever increasingly sophisticated saver and user of capital that can assess risk and trust, this is an unparalleled opportunity for stockbrokers.

A major component of the Financial Services Revolution over the next 30 years that I foresee is that, while the banking regulators are demanding the complete attention of a bank's management during these troubled times, stockbrokers can take away much of the financial intermediation business. By simple disclosure of the risk of an investment and utilization of flexibility provided through communication, the stockbrokers have already taken a huge portion of the Commercial Banks' business away forever. More exciting is the fact that this trend is just getting started.

The regulation handicap that banks and savings institutions are now experiencing is going to handicap them until the year 2000 or further. Everyone believes in fair competition, but few in business would be offended to see their competitors hog-tied, traumatized, and in many ways removed from the competitive playing field of financial commerce for 10 years. The regulation handicap these banks are experiencing could not be occurring at a worse time for the Commercial Banks or at a better time for the stockbrokers.

In the middle of a Technological Communications Revolution, in the middle of a commercial cultural decentralization that is creating revolutionary flexibility, and during the greatest loss of trust and faith since the Great Depression in financial institutions, the banks and savings and loans are being handicapped by the bureaucratic implementation of harsh reactionary 1930's social policy regulation. As the stockbrokers are shifting to utilize financing concepts comparable to the Star Trek mentality of the 21st Century to compete more aggressively, the banks are having the equivalent of their 1950 prop planes grounded for safety inspections for the next 5 to 10 years. Yes, it is a great time for stockbrokers to compete in the Financial Services Industry.

CHANGE SEVEN: THE SELF-RELIANCE OF INVESTORS

This is the last major change causing the Financial Services Revolution. All of the above stated reasons combined with the most educated and self-confident populace in the history of mankind is causing investors to become more self-reliant and knowledgeable.

Investors who utilize discount stockbrokers demonstrate their personal confidence to make financial decisions themselves. The loss of trust in financial institutions is causing a tremendous reassessment and creating the realization of a need to be a self-reliant, enlightened investor in today's and tomorrow's world of finance. That single fact only compounds the accelerating effects of all of the previously mentioned reasons for the Financial Services Revolution. When a housewife can, in the leisure of her home, watch a stock ticker tape, access stock quotes via a personal computer, and electronically execute a trade just as fast or even faster than a professional stockbroker in an office, investors learn to become self-reliant.

SUMMATION OF THE CHANGES WITHIN THE FINANCIAL SERVICES INDUSTRY

The summation of this overview of the Financial Services Industry is to lay before the reader the landscape of the marketplace for the Financial Services Industry for the next 30 years and to describe the players in the Financial Services Industry, their strengths and their weaknesses. Then to reveal to the reader the massive forces and trends of technology, cultural, commerce, and market forces that are moving into or are already in conflict.

The Financial Services Industry is entering the most dynamic phase in its history. The providers of capital are under rapid assault by all of the changes mentioned earlier. Economic history has proven time and time again that in periods of rapid change, the victory always goes to the swiftest. In the case of the Financial Services Business, that would be the stockbroker.

As these rapid changes occur within the United States' Financial Services Industry, the stockbrokerage firms are the swiftest. Even if the other competitors in the Financial Services Business were not being restricted by overzealous regulators demanding 1930's compliance with 21st Century problems, the stockbrokerage industry would win the competition. Every day, the stockbrokerage business is capturing more and more business from its competitors in the Financial Services Business. That trend will continue and expand for the next 30 years.

Stockbrokerage firms today can issue checks, deal in mortgages, fund international trade, accept deposits, issue credit cards, trade car loans, and handle savings and retirement funds for the general public. Remember, that is what they can do now and it's just now the beginning of the "Great Revolution in the Financial Services Industry!"

The Financial Services Industry is entering a revolution that can be analogized to the Transportation Revolution that hit the United States in the 1940's through the 1970's. The railroads, like the banks, were the dominant competitor in their industry. The flexibility of trucking, the speed of air travel, and the flexibility of consumers (both individuals and business) to reassess their needs and wants led to the competitive assault upon the railroads. All of that was compounded by heavy regulation of the railroads by the regulators and their unions to preserve the glory of yesterday's employment and operating traditions. These conditions created an unprecedented shift in the transportation industry.

In 1948, my grandfather could no more grasp the upheaval and revolution that was going to take place in the transportation industry than I can grasp all the evolutionary and revolutionary changes that are going to occur in the Financial Services Business over the next 30 years.

What is different between my grandfather's situation and my own is:

1.   I see the revolution coming, so I remain both open and flexible;

2.   I believe that the stockbrokerage business is the agent of change and stockbrokers are the catalyst of the Financial Services Revolution, and therefore the primary benefactor of the forthcoming upheaval; and

3.   Unlike my grandfather, I plan on being ready for this change and profiting from it.

5

THE STOCKBROKERAGE BUSINESS & THE THREE GREAT WAVES OF THE FUTURE

In the previous chapters, I have stated that I foresee a revolution in the Financial Services Industry during the next 30 years and that Financial Revolution will create a major growth opportunity for the stockbrokerage business. I also believe there are three other major macro-economical and cultural trends occurring which will make the stockbrokerage business a high growth business for the 21st Century. These three "Great Future Waves" are simultaneously dovetailing together. These developments will make the stockbrokerage business one of the fastest growing businesses in the world for the next 30 years.

These three great future wave growth factors are separate from the facts described in Chapter Four. The changes described in Chapter Four basically stated that the stockbrokerage business will, within the Financial Services Industry, be the agent of change and the leader in reshaping the Financial Services Industry over the next 30 years. I believe that the changes within the Financial Services Industry alone will cause growth for the stockbrokerage business. This will occur as stockbrokerage firms win market share away from banks and other providers in the Financial Services Business. Yet, I believe the reasons for the really massive growth in the stockbrokerage business will occur due to the massive marketplace expansion that is going to occur. This massive marketplace need will occur in direct response to the need for stockbrokers over the next 30 years. The opportunity for stockbrokers from the changes in the Financial Services Business will be dwarfed by the convergence of these three massive growth future waves. The opportunity resulting from the three massive macro-economic trends that are occurring will make the stockbrokerage business a very high growth industry for the 21st Century.

GROWTH REASON NUMBER ONE: THE BABY BOOMERS ARE MATURING INTO SAVERS

Every economic forecaster agrees with this simple observation: The portion of our population who were born from 1946 through 1966, generally referred to as the "Baby Boomers," are the largest demographic population wave ever in our society. In the history of what is the developed world, the Baby Boomers are the most massive wave of people ever. The Baby Boomers are not only the largest population wave to flow through our nation or the world, they are also the most educated, the most highly paid, the most affluent, and the least prepared for their financial future.

A brief lesson in economics. Economic theory considers that people pass through certain phases in their life as they age. Childhood is when people are a cost to society. Children generate little economic value to their society in the sense of economic creation. Essentially, we, as a society, invest in our children when they are young with education and other such things. We send them to school instead of to work in the fields as an example.

From the late teens until about age 45, economic theory believes is a period of consumption. Young people start to earn money when they first start to work. Yet, they have tremendous needs and wants to spend their money on. Those needs can be real or perceived. Example: Every teenager has to have a stereo. We can refer to this phase of life, from teenager to the mid-40's, as the consumption phase. Generally, what is earned is spent. It is spent on new cars, new clothes, a home, furniture, having children, buying the children clothes, education for the children, vacations, etc.

It is also during this consumption period that a person is at the lowest earnings of their economical productive life cycle. When you are 23 years old and starting a new job, you are the low person on the totem pole. As a trainee, you are paid accordingly. When you are 35 years old, you have some experience, but you are still junior in the organizational structure of business and paid accordingly. As you approach your mid-40's, you are moving up through the organization with experience and contacts.

Unquestionably, the highest earning period for most people is their late 40's through their early 60's. This is due to the fact that, at this age in life, those people are now taking over the reigns of responsibility and power from the previous generation of managers as the managers retire or pass away

So, during the high consumption phase (ages 18 through 45), people have tremendous needs and wants that they spend their limited earnings upon. At the same time, these people are earning at the lowest point in their over-all lifetime earnings potential because they are the junior trainees. During this consumption phase, people generally spend more money than they earn and therefore make up the difference by borrowing money to pay for their consumption.

The Baby Boomer generation in the United States has lived up to the concept of the consumption phase. No generation in the history of the world has consumed and spent itself into debt like the Baby Boomers.

When the next phase of economic life is reached, age 45 to 65, it is generally referred to as the savings phase because people have generally satisfied their basic living needs. They have a house, furniture, car, the kids are grown, they have enough suits and pairs of shoes and they really do not need to consume that much anymore. What people do see is that their retirement is very close. They realize they need savings to carry them through the next phase of their life - retirement. At age 45, you can easily see that the next 20 years to your retirement could go as fast as the last 20 years, when you were only age 25. This we all understand. As I am approaching the age of 45, I am shocked at how quickly the last 25 years have passed. I am also shocked at how many people are financially ill prepared for retiring and living life after they retire.

Economically speaking, the savings cycle starts at age 45 and continues until retirement. Today, the first of the Baby Boomers population wave are now entering that savings phase of economic life. Those Baby Boomers born in 1946 will be 47 years old in 1993. The largest demographic population wave in the economic history of the world is going to switch from being big consumers to being big savers.

Just now the vanguard of the Baby Boomers group is entering their savings cycle of life. The next 30 years will see the most massive financial readjustment in the history of economics. A study that I recently read reported that it is estimated that in the next 10 years alone the Baby Boomers will save and invest over 6 trillion dollars. To place 6 trillion dollars into perspective, that equals everything invested in the United States since the Pilgrims landed.

This massive wave of population maturing into savers and investors is no secret, everyone with common sense can see the obvious. What is needed to understand the future of commerce and finance is to extend out into the future the continuation of that trend and then to see what it means. Simply, it means that the Baby Boomers will be generating huge amounts of money to save and invest.

It also means that, unlike their parents who did not understand finance and therefore left their savings money passively sitting at the bank for little or no interest, the better educated Baby Boomers are going to demand better investment returns. Therefore, the Baby Boomers are going to need a stockbroker to help them find those returns.

The fact that the Baby Boomers are aging and becoming savers instead of consumers means that the stockbrokerage business will grow rapidly. This major trend is undeniable and massive.

An additional related fact to this massive future wave of the Baby Boomers that should be noted and should not be underestimated is the fact that the Baby Boomers will inherit their parents' wealth. This means that besides the Baby Boomers being the most educated and highest paid population group in the economic history of the world, they will be the first generation to receive their parents' accumulated wealth that has not been ravaged by war or depression.

The parents of the Baby Boomers can be called the Depression Babies or the World War II generation. They inherited little or nothing from their own parents. They had to generate their wealth through the difficulties of depression and then war. Europeans suffered greatly from both the Depression and then World War II and they started in 1946 with nothing. When this generation passes on, they will turn over to their children (the Baby Boomers) their accumulated assets. Those assets will be the greatest transfer of wealth in the economic history of the world between any generations.

Some financially struggling Baby Boomer who has started to realize the importance of savings is beginning to transform from spender to saver. That Baby Boomer will receive the wealth of his or her parents' accumulated wealth through inheritance. This transfer of wealth, undamaged by war or depression, will accelerate the Baby Boomer's massive creation of savings and wealth. All of this means that the Baby Boomers will need stockbrokers as they need to learn how to handle their assets and finances.

Major growth reason number one for the stockbrokerage business over the next 30 years into the 21st Century is that the Baby Boomers are going to become the world's greatest savers and investors. For them to succeed, they are going to need a stockbroker to achieve their financial objectives.

GROWTH REASON NUMBER TWO: THE FAILURE OF BIG BROTHER

The second reason the securities business will be a high growth business over the next 30 years is the failure of "Big Brother." This perception of Big Brother has been sold to all of us by Government and business. By this, I mean that since the middle of the Depression, in the 1930's, Governments and businesses have been telling everyone, "Don't worry about your future financial needs, Big Brother will take care of you."

Whether the concept of Big Brother was Government or business, the message has been the same. We have all been told that this important and powerful entity was going to assure and save us, the simple individuals, from risk or the need to worry about the future. Examples: The United States Government's Social Security System. This program was sold as a retirement insurance program originally. A retirement plan that you have to contribute towards when you are working and when you retire, the Government's retirement system would then care of you forever. Another example is the Federal Government told savers that if they placed their savings deposit with a certain bank, the Federal Government would insure them from losses.

The Federal Government has promised us that it will take care of us in so many ways that it has become like our benevolent and generous Big Brother. A Big Brother that is going to take care of us so we do not have to worry about anything. The Federal Government has promised retirement care, health care, pension guarantees, farm guarantees, educational guarantees, job guarantees, and more.

This era of the perception that Big Brother would be taking care of us was also provided by different states in the United States. These states offered similar programs such as health care, welfare care, bank and insurance guarantees, job guarantees, and more. Not to be left out of the Big Brother promises are counties, cities, school districts, and unions which all also wanted to act as the all-caring, all-powerful Big Brother. They promised they would take care of us and we did not need to worry about saving and investing for our retirement or emergencies. Everyone was saying don't worry because someone was going to take care of us.

Big business, not wanting to be left behind on the Big Brother concept, either volunteered or was coerced into acting as the all powerful Big Brother. Businesses did this through pension fund promises that included lifetime medical care, death benefits, retirement, and more.

For the last 50 years, all levels of Government and business have been telling people, "Don't worry, Big Brother is going to take care of you when you retire." Now, the reality of the unfunded pension programs, the run-away cost of health care, and the unbearable financial burden that those promises placed upon the economics of our society are becoming a reality. The reality is that we, the recipients, will never receive what they have promised us. This fact is coming home to everyone's attention. Yes, we all have good reason to worry about our futures. The fact that no one else is really going to take care of us is now starting to come home for most people.

Few Baby Boomers believe the Social Security System will give them anything in their retirement or that whatever they receive will not be nearly enough. Major companies are now modifying their promises to retirees and future retirees. Cities and school districts are discovering they are spending more on their health care and retirement benefits for retired workers than they are spending on their primary mission of educating children. Savings depositors have learned that Federal Insurance is not a panacea to irresponsible bank managers and that they have to worry about who they deposit with. In plain words, everyone is learning that the promise made by all levels of Government and business of, "Don't worry, we are going to take care of you tomorrow," is hollow and empty.

Every day, more and more people are waking up to the cruel reality that they must take care of themselves financially. People are realizing they must save and invest and be self-assured that they will be able to financially retire. People are realizing that their financial security will be from their own efforts and not from some large, faceless body that promises more than it can deliver.

Yes, people are realizing that Governments, big companies, cities, unions, and others are breaking their promises of financial paradise. These institutions are laying off people, renegotiating contracts, going bankrupt to avoid paying pension promises, removing money from pension plans or have not adequately funded their pension promises in the first place. Yes, people are realizing that Big Brother cannot or will not be able to take care of them. That means they must then take care of themselves.

The average person is now realizing that Big Brother, whether Government or business, is not going to solve all their financial problems for them. In fact, Big Brother may cause the people more problems by its failure to perform as promised. The failure of this concept of Big Brother and that someone else is going to take care of us, means that people of all age groups are realizing that they must take care of themselves financially. What self-reliance means in the financial world is, as millions of people are realizing, they must take care of themselves, and save and invest for tomorrow. To do that, they will all be needing a stockbroker!

Fifty years ago, only the rich needed stockbrokers. Today, the middle class needs stockbrokers and in 20 years even the poor will need stockbrokers. Everyone will need stockbrokers to explain, educate, and assist them in their own financial self-reliance. In taking care of themselves and their families, savers will be turning to stockbrokers in massive numbers. As the average person is awakening to the failure of the Socialist promise that someone else will take care of you, he or she will realize what they need is a stockbroker to help them take care of themselves financially for emergencies, retirement, or just a real piece of mind.

The second reason that the securities business will be a high growth business into the 21st Century is the failure of the concept of Big Brother to take care of us. That failed promise means we must all take care of ourselves financially and for that we will all need the help of a stockbroker.

GROWTH REASON NUMBER THREE: THE REAL BEGINNING OF WORLD CAPITALISM

The third reason the stockbrokerage business is a high growth business is the most exciting of all - The Real Beginning of World Capitalism.

In 1980, 4 out of 5 people on the face of the earth were not free to be Capitalist. Communism, Socialism, Central Planning, Dictatorships, The Guiding Hand, or whatever you want to call it, did not allow people to pursue their own economic betterment. Over 80% of the human beings on the earth were not free to economically prosper by starting a business, saving, investing, borrowing, buying shares, or making investments into their future or the future of their children.

During the 1980's, the Third World Debt Crisis forced nations to default upon their bank loans. First, Latin American nations and then the countries of Africa defaulted on their bank debts. With the defaulting of their debts, those countries were then ostracized by the world's financial communities.

Faced with a financial boycott by the Capitalists of the financial capitals of the world, mostly because of their commercial and economic unattractiveness, nations in Latin America were forced to abandon their Elitist economic policies and return to the legitimate world of Free Market Economics. Chile, Mexico, Columbia, Venezuela, Bolivia, and Argentina are all returning to the world of open Free Market Economics known as Capitalism. Some countries in Latin America still need to realize the economic and human horror of their Elitist economic policies of the past and return to Free Market Economics.

In Africa, the commercial process is slowly returning to the Free Market Economics of Capitalism. This is occurring throughout Africa, albeit at a delayed and sporadic manner with much leaping and wrenching back and forth. Every day, African nations are becoming more and more knowledgeable about the reality of what economic policies create wealth for the citizens of their nations. Every day, African nations are turning rapidly to Free Market Economic policies that have been proven to create a better life for all.

Most countries in Eastern Europe and what used to be the Soviet Union are now actively pursuing Free Market Economics. Some countries have accepted the concept on a pure basis and others are still seeking a middle road. Eventually, results will prove that there is no such thing as half-free markets and Eastern Europe and the former Soviet Union will, within 20 years, be pure Free Market Economic Systems.

Half of Asia is open to Free Market Economics. It is interesting to observe that every nation in Asia that they call a "rich nation" has Free Market Economics. Half of Asia's nations are still closed to Free Market Economics with Communist and Elitist economic policies. Interesting again to note that all of those nations are known as the "poor nations" of Asia. The populations of the Asian nations are noticing the harsh realities between those nations that are improving the lives of their citizens and those that are not. Slowly, the Governments of the remaining nations of Asia are accepting the economic reality that people free to create wealth, do so and prosper.

This world-wide political acceptance of the economic truth that Free Market Capitalism is the only way for the nations of the world to proceed is slowly coming about. What that means is that Capitalism is going to have, by the year 2000, four and a half billion new participants. That's right, 4.5 billion new Capitalists in the world, an increase of over 400% in the next 8 years. Four and a half billion people who want a better life and now can do something about it, such as start a business, invest in a shop, develop a company, hire people to work, and improve the lives of themselves and those around them by being free to commerce with others. Four and a half billion people that have needs and wants. They need health care, education, clothing, shelter, and more. They want a better life, a television, radio, refrigerator, car, air conditioner, VCR, telephone, trip to Hawaii, and on and on. Four and a half billion people that will stimulate the world's economy in ways we cannot even imagine. These people will need distribution companies, manufacturing companies, service companies, and, most important of all, they will need stockbrokers.

That's right, stockbrokers. How can you enter the world of Capitalism without its most important profession in the world of commerce, stockbrokers? The answer is that you cannot. To gather the surplus capital and place it where it is best utilized will become a massive and growing business. This is the most massive and powerful of the three trends that we have discussed. These three trends are going to drive the stockbrokerage business, over the next 30 years, as an incredibly high growth business.

SUMMATION OF THE FUTURE TRENDS FROM THESE THREE MASSIVE WAVES

First, look at the massive forces that are creating these trends that we are talking about here. Then, take those trends and extend them out over the next 30 years and this leads us to these observations:

First: The Baby Boomers need to save and invest for their retirement. Within the next 10 years, an estimated 6 trillion dollars will be saved and invested. Twenty years after that, even more. Trillions of dollars of savings needing to be invested.

<u>Second</u>: The Baby Boomers and others cannot trust Government and others to take care of them, so they will handle and invest their own money. They will seek the best possible investment returns available. Due to their enlightenment and their need to catch up on their retirement pool, the Baby Boomers will be more receptive to new, higher earning opportunities.

<u>Third</u>: The rest of the world, with 4.5 billion people, has just come along with decades of pent-up consumer demand and no capital to create a better society for themselves or their children.

The merging of all three of these trends is obvious. The trillions of dollars that are going to be saved in the developed world by the Baby Boomers are not needed there anymore. We do not need any more office buildings in Los Angeles (for 6 years at least) or any more shopping malls or x, or y, or z. As the Baby Boomers save trillions of dollars of surplus capital, the developed world will generate capital surpluses far in excess of its needs. It is possible that, in the future, United States investors will look at today's 3% interest rates as high rates of return when compared to the rates of returns from investments available to them in the United States then.

So what will happen? The obvious is that the developing world will bid for the surplus capital of the already developed world and build themselves a better and richer world. These 4.5 billion people will borrow or attract capital to build cities, water systems, hospitals, power plants, roads, telephones, schools, and much more. United States industry will become the source of goods and services for the rest of the world, all financed by the Baby Boomers' savings pools. Prosperity previously unimagined will become a realization as everyone participates in a better world. The secret to this dramatic worldwide commercial and economic growth is financial capital brought to you by stockbrokers, stockbrokers in the United States and everywhere else in the world servicing the savers and users of capital.

Already in the United States, capital markets are seeing many non-U.S. companies raising capital within the borders of the United States to finance their development. These securities offerings are called "Yankee Equities" and they will be the biggest business of the next 30 years in the securities industry. Look at the obvious trends: We have capital and they want it. From 1987 until 1992, the two best performing stocks on the New York Stock Exchange in the United States were:

#1   Telephones de Mexico

#2   Philippine Long Distance

That's right, and thousands of Americans have made money on these two companies and are looking for more like them. I have seen the future and it is us "stockbrokers" financing and serving the development of the world.

Before I conclude this section on the reasons why the stockbrokerage business will be a high growth business for the next 30 years, it is important to expand upon one other undeniable fact again. The United States is the world's technological leader in Capitalism. There are many industries in which the United States claims to be the technological leader: space, communications, medicine, computers, etc. Yet, without question, the United States leads the world in the technology of how to implement Capitalism: equity capital, venture capital, public issues, municipal financing, debt, options, deviates, futures, trading, exchanging, and others are all dominated by the United States stockbroker technology.

This leadership in Capitalism has also made the United States businesses the leaders in entrepreneurship. When you have aggressive and risk oriented capital markets, then you also foster the new enterprises and entrepreneurs that result from that capital formation. This leadership in Capitalism in the United States has created a need for legal structures that support both the ease of capital formation and aftermarket trading. The resulting capital markets generate liquidity and even greater capital markets. Legal development to service the capital markets goes hand-in-hand with the development of accounting standards and accounting treatments that generate greater comfort to investors about full and fair disclosure. All of these factors together develop an investment climate of full disclosure and adequate risk assessment. The basic infrastructure of capital markets, legal, accounting, entrepreneurship, and banking have all combined to support the technology that is America's capital market technology leadership.

All of this capital market leadership supports the most advanced capital markets industry in the world. The distribution of securities as a part of the system of capital markets is almost unknown outside of the United States. Securities wholesalers are almost nonexistent outside of the United States and Britain. The exchange of shares and bonds is an American art form.

The National Association of Securities Dealers Automatic Quotation System (NASDAQ) is a computer networking based trading and exchange system. This computer system allows all securities firms that are NASDAQ members direct access to any securities of their choosing by simply sitting at a computer terminal and pressing a few keys. No stock exchange in the world can rival the NASDAQ trading system when it comes to decentralization of data and opportunity. The reality is that part of the commercial greatness of the United States derives from its capital markets. The development of the United States venture capital markets and its new companies development rests directly with the fact that regional companies and enterprises have equal access to the capital markets of the United States, as any company based in New York City. The NASDAQ trading system is revolutionizing the world and it is just getting started internationally. I predict that in 20 years the NASDAQ trading system will be the world's primary stock and bond exchange.

Researching companies is one of the areas of technological leadership of United States stockbrokers. This has to be considered the area of American stockbrokers "high ground." United States stockbrokers do more real research on companies and their prospects than any other nations' stockbrokers proportionally by a factor of 10. American stockbrokers seek out undervalued investment situations. Stock analysts risk their reputations to be different from everyone else in the pursuit of better investing. More importantly, I see that information gap widening, not shrinking, as other nations are trying to restrict research.

The most important part of the United States' capital markets leadership is the requirement of fairness to the investors. While no system is perfect and there will always be dishonesty where there are large sums of money involved, the reality is that the United States securities markets are the fairest in the world and that is part of their technological leadership. For capital markets to develop and prosper, the investors must believe that they are being treated fairly. For all of its many shortcomings, the United States and its stockbrokers believe that investors must receive fairness. That is what provides the United States capital markets their amazing depth of investors and liquidity.

In conclusion of this chapter, the facts are overwhelming that the three macro-economic trends of the aging of the Baby Boomers, the failure of the concept of Big Brother, and the dawning of the age of internationalization of Capitalism means that the stockbrokerage business is about to begin the greatest growth phase in its history.

For the next 30 years, the stockbrokerage business will grow in ways unimagined today. This tremendous world economic and commercial growth will be led and developed by the United States stockbrokers. This is because the stockbrokers of the United States are the technological leaders by 20 years over second place England. The world's developing capital markets will turn to the United States stockbrokers for help in their capital markets' development. Those nations that do not seek United States stockbrokers help in developing their nations' capital markets will lose the economic race in the new age for international capital market development. This will mean that their citizens will suffer slow economic development and stagnation due to a lack of capital in the Free Market Capitalist System that the world has accepted today. This also means that citizens of those nations will replace the leaders who do not let them improve their lives.

The stockbrokerage business is a high growth industry with an extremely bright future for at least the next 30 years and it will be led by the United States stockbrokers. The greatest business in the world is the stockbrokerage business and it will be one of the fastest growing business in the world, especially for those that have international contacts and services that the new world–wide Capitalist will need.

6

THE REVOLUTION OCCURRING WITHIN THE STOCKBROKERAGE INDUSTRY

We are basically half-way through this book. We have discussed what a stockbroker is, and a brief description of the Financial Services Industry today. We then projected the Financial Services Industry of tomorrow and the three waves and reasons why the stockbrokerage business is a high growth business for at least the next 30 years. The first half of this book has been focused at the massive macro–economic, technological and cultural trends that are going to sweep the stockbrokerage business forward into the 21st Century. All of these factors will act like a huge tidal wave carrying the stockbrokerage business forward as a New Wave of international commercial change.

While I foresee many rapid changes affecting the marketplace of financial services and that those changes are giving the stockbrokers a competitive advantage, the stockbrokerage business itself will not be immune from its own internal revolution created by these same forces. This chapter will focus upon the internal revolution occurring within the stockbrokerage business as it evolves into the 21st Century.

In 1975, the United States securities industry deregulated. This was the start of the first great revolution within the securities industry. Today, a short 15 years later, the securities industry has changed considerably. Stockbrokerage firms such as Charles Schwab, Quick and Reily, and others have created a whole new segment of the stockbrokerage industry referred to as "Discount Stockbrokers." Firms such as Edward D. Jones and Thomas James have developed magnificent profitable niches in the securities business that were not even perceived of in 1975 as being viable.

Just as these firms developed niches within the stockbrokerage industry over the last 15 years, I see similar new niches developing within the stockbrokerage business in the future. New niches within the stockbrokerage business that can be as big and profitable as the original creation of the Discount Stockbrokerage segment of the brokerage business.

These new niches developing within the stockbrokerage business are resulting from the massive trends and changes discussed earlier. These new areas will grow and develop over the next 30 years. I believe some of these niches will become so large as to become a major part of the securities business by the year 2020. The 21st Century Stockbroker that I foresee will be very different from the stockbroker we know today.

While I believe that the securities business will be the agent of much of the change in the financial services marketplace, I also believe that the securities business itself will be undergoing rapid change. Earlier, I discussed how the Communications and Computer Revolutions have affected the Financial Services Business. Equally true is the fact that these two revolutions, along with a third revolution, are going to change the stockbrokerage business. The third factor is lifestyle.

The stockbrokerage business, similar to most businesses, has become centralized. Historically, the stockbrokers of the world traveled to their offices where they centralized the flow of money capital through their hands. This has historically been due to the reality that communications and accounting controls demanded such a centralized system.

Historically, stockbrokers were recruited from the best families and attended the best schools. Stockbrokers were recruited as much for who they were as for what they were. This led to the stockbrokerage business being the most elite of all businesses. Only the rich had stockbrokers and only a rich man's son could become a stockbroker. This is still the situation in most of the world's stock markets today.

Fortunately, that situation has changed in the United States. The change started in the mid-60's. So many new industries were being created in the United States that new opportunities were being created for everyone. To understand those new industries, Wall Street needed people with specific technological knowledge of those industries. That technical knowledge had to be learned and was not inherited. An example: In 1968, when I started in the stockbrokerage business, my personal break occurred because of computers. Computers were a completely new business area for Wall Street. The stockbrokerage establishment did not know computers and they looked for young men with some computer background to show them the way. I was one of those young men. When I arrived in 1968, I started studying computers and computer companies. I was fortunate to be in the right place at the right time, in southern California where the computer industry was booming, strong, and dynamic. I became an expert on mini-computers when no one else wanted to learn them. When a new computer company in southern California wanted to raise investors' capital so that they could expand, I was often part of the evaluation and corporate finance team that reviewed them. This was because I was perceived as one of our computer experts.

So in the 1960's, the stockbrokerage business started to open up to others than the sons of the rich elite. The stockbrokerage business needed people with technical knowledge and the rich elite did not possess it, so Wall Street recruited it.

Then another opportunity was created later in the 1970's. The Mutual Fund Industry started to really grow and develop. All of a sudden, Wall Street learned that a regular person out gathering financial assets for them to manage was good business. Stockbrokers learned that besides the son of a wealthy man being a stockbroker to other rich people who he knew at the country club, a blue collar type of person collecting investment funds from his buddies at work was big business and very profitable to Wall Street. This commercial evolution I refer to as the "democratization of the United States capital markets." The business of gathering assets for the capital markets started in the 1960's. Yet the Mutual Fund Industry truly gathered steam and developed its massive marketplace niche in the 1970's and 1980's.

This marketplace niche that the Mutual Funds have developed is very different from the traditional 1950's stockbroker. This democratization of the stockbrokerage business is so new that some stockbrokerage firms have only recently developed its true concept in the last 15 years. That is, stockbrokerage firms that just focus to serve the niche of gathering assets for the mutual fund marketplace niche of the securities business.

Today, within the stockbrokerage business in the United States, we have seen this specialized niche develop. A niche where stockbrokerage firms have few traditional stockbrokers trading stocks, but firms that have stockbrokers who are primarily "asset gatherers." These asset gatherers do not manage customers, pick investments, or deal in stocks and bonds. Most stockbrokerage firms referred to as Financial Planners would fit into this category.

The 1975 financial deregulation changed the Wall Street "old boys club" into open, fierce, cut-throat competition. This deregulation allowed discount commissions, thereby creating the Discount Stockbrokerage firms, a new business niche in 1975. The effects of the "declubbing" of Wall Street are still being felt in the United States capital markets. These effects have yet to get started anywhere else in the world's capital markets. This opening of the United States capital markets to everyone was the beginning of commercial democratization of the United States capital markets. It basically allowed everyone with the passion to become stockbrokers in the United States the opportunity. The stockbrokerage industry was now free to compete, innovate, and create.

The deregulation of the stockbrokerage business in 1975 released tremendous amounts of creative genius for the securities industry's benefit. The effects of this freedom to innovate and create new marketplace niches within the securities business are still continuing today. What I envision as the 21st Century Stockbroker will be the results of the continuation of this evolution of the stockbroker into tomorrow.

While this democratizing of the United States capital markets is occurring, another major trend will affect the United States securities industry for the next 30 years. That other major trend is the greatest immigration wave in the history of the United States. Millions of people every year have immigrated to the United States over the last 25 years and millions more will continue to immigrate here.

Unlike the previous wave of immigrants that came to the United States at the turn of the Century, this wave of immigrants was not poor and downtrodden. These immigrants today include medical doctors from the Philippines, India, Eastern Europe, and Latin America, and business people of Asia, Africa, and Europe, many fleeing Communism or its brother, Socialism.

This New Wave of immigrants to the United States are educated, experienced, and in many cases, wealthy. Most important about these new immigrants is that they are commercially hungry for a better life for themselves and their family. In many cases, members of their family remain in their former homeland. This has led to the development of a commercial aspect for the United States stockbrokerage business for ethnic opportunities. Each of these immigrant nationalities within the United States offers a unique and interesting business opportunity for the United States stockbrokerage business.

Since the deregulation of the stockbrokerage business in 1975, many new niches have developed within the securities business. The traditional stockbrokerage firm has been under continuous assault by these pesky new firms developing these new marketplace niches. These new marketplace niches being developed by the new stockbrokerage firms is the stockbrokerage business that the traditional stockbrokerage firms cannot or will not serve. The traditional stockbrokerage firm is also under assault from the same future trends that I mentioned earlier. Similar to everyone in the Financial Services Industry, the traditional stockbrokerage firm is faced with a rapidly changing marketplace. Traditional stockbrokerage firms such as E.F.Hutton, Glore Forgan, Hornblower, and Blyth are gone forever. New names such as Charles Schwab, Quick and Reily, Thomas James and Edward D. Jones are moving up the rankings of stockbrokerage firms. These are stockbrokerage firms that are developing new niches within the stockbrokerage business.

What does the future hold for the 21st Century Stockbroker? A new group of stockbrokerage firms serving new and very specialized marketplace niches within the securities industry. This will all lead to an opening up and further democratization of the United States capital markets. These trends that I speak about are not maturing trends, they are emerging, accelerating trends. We are just now starting to see the beginning of the second revolution within the stockbrokerage business itself.

The primary issue that needs to be understood by the reader here is that the United States stockbrokerage business is still undergoing rapid change within itself. All of the trends mentioned earlier in this book are creating new marketplace niches for the stockbrokerage business and new business opportunities to service them. The trends that are occurring now are accelerating their affect upon the stockbrokerage business. The second revolution within the stockbrokerage business is just now beginning and it will continue for the next 30 years. Ethnic markets, communications, computers, and lifestyle changes are all modifying the stockbrokerage business, modifying the business beyond the wildest dreams of the 1950's stockbrokers. The changes that are occurring and will continue to occur will cause the revolution of the Financial Services Business into the 21st Century.

THE THREE MAJOR NEW NICHE MARKETS FOR THE 21ST CENTURY STOCKBROKER

Writing about the concept of future change is very easy. Being specific about what business changes will occur is much more difficult. The balance of this chapter is going to be utilized to explore the three major new niche markets that I foresee within the securities business and the associated business opportunities. These will be the major new business opportunities for the stockbrokerage business as it moves towards the 21st Century. A reader may ask, "Will these new business opportunities for the stockbrokerage business be as big as the discount stockbrokers were 15 years ago?" I think the answer is yes!

The three major new opportunities in the stockbrokerage business into the 21st Century will be:

1. Ethic Markets
2. Decentralization
3. Lifestyle Changes

We will explore each of these topics briefly so the reader can appreciate my reasoning.

1.   Ethnic Markets for the Stockbrokerage Business

There is no doubt in my mind that one of the greatest and most exciting areas of opportunity in the stockbrokerage business today is the ethnic markets.

Originally, the realization of the huge business potential of this new niche in the securities marketplace dawned upon me in the fall of 1991. At that time, I took over as the President of the operations of a securities firm which had over 1,300 stockbrokers based in southern California. As we, the new management team of the company, developed a better understanding of the ethnic make-up of the people of this stockbrokerage firm, I realized the opportunity. We discovered that 82 of the company's stockbrokers were Filipino-Americans, another 104 were Indian-American, and there were many Chinese, Taiwanese, Koreans, Thailanders, Russians, Poles, and more. This ethnic data about the make-up of the nationality of the stockbrokers of this firm blended with my many years of international investment banking activity. This realization opened up my mind to the business possibilities.

For many years, I have been a consultant engaged in advising developing nations about how they should develop their domestic capital markets. The area of development of the capital markets of the developing world is one of my personal pet projects. I have spent countless months overseas working in this area to develop the viability of capital markets development in the developing world. I personally believe that this is one of the most tremendous business opportunity for the next 30 years.

As part of my efforts to educate the leaders of these developing nations on what they must do to develop their nations' full economic potential, I advocate that first they must develop their domestic capital markets. Over the last 5 years, I have given seminars in 48 countries around the world, from Russia to India, to Africa, to Latin America, on how to develop capital markets. Always, I would tell the country's leaders that the main component of their capital market's development was the development of a domestic distribution system for securities within their nation. Everywhere that I gave my lectures on how to develop capital markets, I emphasized that without distribution systems for securities, you cannot have capital markets develop that are viable. This has been the main emphasis of my speeches in all 48 countries that I have spoken in: <u>You must develop your capital markets distribution systems or you will not succeed in developing your capital markets</u>.

Given that working with these developing nations has been the center of my efforts for the last 5 years, I started to realize what the business opportunities might be when I was reviewing the make-up of the stockbrokers of the firm I had just taken over as President. I had my staff at the firm provide me with the personal background data on all 1,300 stockbrokers in the firm. It became obvious to me that we had one of the largest ethnic stockbrokerage sales force in the world. We had more Filipinos as stockbrokers in that firm than all of the stockbrokerage firms in the Philippines combined! The same was true of Indians, Nigerians, Russians, Chinese, etc. We were, by accident, the largest securities distribution system for those developing nations already. I then realized that Montano Securities had greater securities distribution power for the capital markets of those developing countries in the United States already than those developing countries had within their own borders.

Additional investigation revealed to me that these ethnic stockbrokers' clientele were mostly comprised of the stockbrokers' own immigrant nationality. For example, Russian-Americans were perhaps 80% of the Russian-American stockbroker's clientele, the Indian-American stockbroker's clients were mostly made up of other Indian-Americans, and so forth. From this, I analyzed the tremendous new marketplace niche available for the future stock market development. The business potential is extremely great.

Most people in the United States will think when I say ethnic markets of those historical and primary ethnic markets in the United States, such as African, Mexican, and Puerto Rican. That is the traditional mindset of what is normally defined as "ethnic" in the United States. And yes, those are excellent business opportunities since they are extremely underserved in the United States' securities markets today.

For illustration, let's discuss the African-American ethnic market. By my crude estimate, the traditional African-American ethnic securities marketplace opportunity in the United States has only been developed to about 20% of its marketplace potential today. Since I believe in the Financial Services Revolution that I am predicting over the next 30 years, I believe the stockbrokerage industry will grow by expanding and taking market share away from banks and savings organizations in this traditional ethnic marketplace. This will be especially true in what is traditionally defined as the ethnic marketplace in the United States. I believe the traditional ethnic marketplace opportunity for the stockbrokerage business will increase by over 300% in the next 30 years.

If I am correct, then for the traditional African-American marketplace in the United States, the growth potential over the next 30 years should be tremendous. Since I project the overall marketplace potential for servicing the needs of the African-American savers and investors in the United States will grow 300% in the next 30 years and that the present marketplace of African-American savers and investors is only 20% served today, I believe you could see a 1500% growth in the amount of African-American business in the securities business over the next 30 years.

That magnitude of substantial growth is possible in all of the major ethnic groups in the United States. Increases of 10 to 20 times the present levels of securities business in most of the major United States ethnic markets is easy to forecast. At the present time, the United States domestic financial markets are dramatically underserving these traditional ethnic marketplaces within the United States.

There is a combination of reasons for this underserving of the traditional ethnic marketplace. First, the old Elitist habits of the 1950's stockbrokerage industry. Second, the failure of ethnics to enter the securities business. Third, the failure of everyone to educate and communicate to these communities the advantages of securities investing. Educating the traditional ethnic savers and investors about the advantages of the securities market will be the primary cause for growth within the marketplace.

Yet I believe that in the United States today there are two ethnic marketplaces. One ethnic marketplace is Americans of African descent, those who have been in the United States for several generations and their home base is the United States. The other ethnic marketplace are African-Americans, those that have been in the United States only as first generation immigrants. Hundreds of thousands of people from African nations have fled their former homes to seek a better life in the United States, people from Nigeria, The Ivory Coast, Ghana, Senegal, etc. These people have two potential securities markets to serve. One is the United States' domestic markets of their fellow new immigrants and the other is the securities market opportunity of their former homeland, a homeland where they still have friends and contacts.

As the Capitalism Revolution sweeps around the world, these new immigrants to the United States have an opportunity to help lead the capital markets development of their former homelands. These immigrants can lead the development of the capital markets of their former homelands into the future and make huge personal profits in the process.

I was recently informed that from Ghana alone, over 300,000 people now reside within the United States. Many of these Ghana immigrants are medical doctors and technology specialists. Here is a small example of the opportunity that I am addressing: A Ghanian-American can become a United States stockbroker. He can service the Ghanese community within the United States and introduce financial services and investment products to them. That effort will enhance their investment yields over competing banks and other financial services providers. He can also position himself to participate in the reopening of Ghana to the world's capital markets.

The best example of these new business opportunities for the securities business that I can provide is the Philippines. The United States has had a special relationship with the Philippines for over 90 years. I estimate there are over 3 million Filipino-Americans living within the United States today. Most of the Filipino-Americans are not familiar with the concepts of the securities markets and they are therefore underinvested and underserved.

These Filipino-Americans have billions of dollars of savings in the United States at the Commercial Banks earning, at this time, 3% in time deposits. As more and more Filipino-Americans become stockbrokers in the United States, they are educating their fellow Filipino-Americans on the advantages of securities market investing. These Filipino-American investors are discovering that they can move their savings from an account at Bank of America, where it earns 3%, into Bank of America Bonds and earn 8.2%. The same company, Bank of America, and, in reality, about the same risk. "Yes, that's right," says the new Filipino-American stockbroker to his fellow Filipinos, "you can earn over 200% more from the same company by utilizing a stockbroker instead of a banker for investing your savings." Now this is a huge marketplace opportunity itself for Filipino-Americans within the United States.

Equally true is that the Philippines, like many developing countries, has an underdeveloped capital market. That means generally that the primary source of capital for development or business expansion are the Commercial Banks. The Commercial Banks in the Philippines are very profitable and very selective about whom they allocate capital to. Example: In the Philippines, in November 1992, a fully secured home mortgage loan is charged about 24% annual interest. That's right, a Filipino must make a 30% down payment for the purchase of a home and then if (and that is a big if) he or she can get a mortgage loan from a bank, the rate will be 24% per year.

Now, the Ghanese-American in New York has no interest in investing his money in the Philippines. He has read in the newspaper that the Philippines is a poor and confused country. But the Filipino-American stockbroker knows this is not true. The Philippines has not yet fallen off the face of the earth and there are no indications from his relatives back in the Philippines that things are all that bad. He knows that some of his Filipino-American clients can accept the business risk of investing in the Philippines' mortgages. The United States' Filipino-American stockbroker has analyzed the risk-to-rewards ratio and he finds it is very favorable for investment. This is especially true given the Filipino-American's enhanced knowledge of the true risk of the Philippines.

If some of these Filipino-Americans moved some of their money into a Philippine Mortgage Investment Trust yielding 24%, they could be very happy investors. For those of you reading this book without a calculator, that's almost 8 times more investment return than their interest at Bank of America in the savings account.

Yes, there is more risk. Eight times more risk? No. Calculate that $25,000 left in savings at 3% will in 20 years be worth $36,122. Then calculate that $25,000 earning 24% for the same 20 years which will equal $1,477,283. That is big money.

The ethnic immigrant opportunities exist both domestically in the United States and internationally. Here is a short and incomplete list just to awaken your imagination of this business potential:

(Alphabetically by continent)

Africa: Nigeria, Ghana, Ivory Coast, Senegal, Kenya, South Africa, Egypt, and more;

Latin America: Mexico, Central America, Argentina, Brazil, and more;

Asia: Philippines, Japan, Korea, China, Taiwan, Indonesia, Malaysia, Thailand, India, Pakistan, Sri Lanka, Hong Kong, and more; and

Europe: Russia, Poland, Ukraine, Romania, Turkey, Bulgaria, Hungary, and more.

We are at the dawning of a new age in world Capitalism and we in the United States can prosper beyond our wildest dreams from this unique opportunity. We are standing at the door of the greatest worldwide economic expansion in the history of mankind. The developing world needs investment capital desperately and is willing to pay 24% returns and more because they need capital for development.

America and its new immigrant ethnic communities have surplus capital. What a business opportunity. What a real world chance to get rich and make the world a better place while you are doing it. Yes, this is one of the areas of the Stockbrokerage Revolution of the 21st Century for stockbrokers that I love and believe in. The dawning of world Capitalism funded by the ethnic American communities all handled by United States based stockbrokers.

This subject is covered in greater detail in Chapter Nine of this book.

2. The Decentralization of the Stockbrokerage Business

One of the major changes that I foresee occurring in the stockbrokerage business in the United States during the next 30 years is the dramatic decentralization of the business. Earlier in this book, I talked about how Wall Street was the gathering place for those who controlled and transacted in capital. Given the travel modes of the 19th Century, providers of capital had to physically live close together to succeed.

In 1900, it took almost a week to cross from New York to California. The only real form of communications then was telegraph which, at best, was cryptic and brief, and did not allow for two-way communication to clarify understanding.

Imagine in 1900, you had to visit a company in California and you lived in New York. You boarded the train and traveled for a week with no air conditioning, no radio, no TV, only reading material and limited amounts of that, and great physical and emotional discomfort as toilets were a luxury, food was suspect, and sleeping was cramped and shaky. You are going to the barbaric and savage City of Los Angeles which, if it had a hotel, you knew it was basic at best. Medical care, telephones calls to the family, and other such conveniences were not even conceivable.

After staying in Los Angeles a week and reading the reports presented to you by the company you are visiting (handwritten, of course), you make a decision that this might be a good investment for your firm's clients' capital. You then travel a week back to New York and have to convince your partners in New York that California will not fall into the sea or have a civil war. Three weeks of hard and difficult work in the field just to return and attempt to overcome both the ignorance of your partners and their reluctance to invest in this dangerous and distant place.

Now it is 1993. You are in New York and a California company wants you to invest in their company. First, the California company sends you their reports and proposals via fax and Federal Express. You review and discuss the data with your partners. You then have a 2 hour telephone conference meeting with the company's management in California. After agreeing to the basic concepts of the investment project, you decide to go to Los Angeles.

You jump on a 7:00 a.m. (E.S.T.) flight at New York airport to Los Angeles and arrive at 10:00 a.m. (P.S.T.). The company's management picks you up at the airport and take you to a first class hotel. A hotel with TV, radios, telephones, and more, such as exercise facilities, nightclubs, restaurants, etc. Oh yes, I forgot, during the airplane ride you had a computer to work on in your lap, watched a movie, and used the telephone on the plane to check in with the office.

After you check into the hotel, you are taken out to the company where you are given a video presentation and then a tour of the company. At 3:00 p.m. that day, you call you partners in New York and discuss your ideas. You then have more discussions with the company's management at 4:00 P.M. before they take you to a gourmet restaurant for dinner.

That night, you call your family from the hotel, watch TV, and maybe a movie, and then go to sleep. Next morning, you are on a 7:00 a.m. flight home to New York and you have dinner in your own home and sleep in your own bed. One night away from home, great comfort, and the next day you are showing your partners the company's video which visualizes the situation to them.

Yes, the Communications Revolution is just getting starting towards the decentralization of finance in the United States. This small example also means that very smart stockbrokers do not have to go into New York City to be in the securities business. I know of one stockbroker who has a NASDAQ trading system in the bedroom of his home on the beach in California where he works every day. He can, through computer networking, participate as actively in the securities markets as anyone on Wall Street.

This decentralization of the stockbrokerage business is resulting from the Communications Revolution and the Transportation Revolution. What the effect of this decentralization of data and communications power means is that human relationships will matter more than ever in the financial world in the future.

People in San Diego, Seattle, or Houston can all have an intimate relationship with a stockbroker in Boston. More importantly, a retired person in Arizona can have a very personal relationship with a stockbroker just down the street. The retiree knows that the stockbroker just down the street has the same access to the investment products and the capital markets as any stockbroker in New York City.

All this means that very personal relationships can be developed between customers and stockbrokers in the future. Trust, confidence, and personal knowledge are all possible for the potential investor. Now, because the Communications Revolution allows the world to integrate through networking, stockbrokers can become much more personable.

In the future, a stockbroker could be out on the golf course every day playing golf with his customers. If the office needs him or there is a change of circumstances that requires his immediate attention, the office can call the stockbroker on his cellular phone. If an important letter comes into the office, just fax it to him on his portable fax in the golf cart. A special investment need from a customer? Easy, patch the stockbroker through to the research specialist in Omaha, Nebraska and the other specialist who is on a cruise ship in the Mediterranean. Yes, the days of the Communications Revolution are just now beginning and their affects upon the stockbrokerage business are just now being felt.

As this decentralization of the stockbrokerage business takes place, more and more personal relationship can be created. Distances will shrink and information will transfer more freely allowing for greater awareness and greater freedom.

The greatest freedom to investors will be caused by enlightenment through education of so many people about their personal investing. This will ease the fears of many about investing as they learn more about the process. The fear of investing has a potential stockbroker's clients leaving their money in the bank earning very low rates of returns. Why? Out of fear that bonds from the same bank are somehow mystical and therefore, more dangerous. The same fear has people depositing their savings into a bank to earn low interest rates while ignoring an investment yield 3 times greater from a AAA rated Preferred Stock from the same bank. The Information Revolution will open the door for so many people who have wasted investment earnings power out of fear caused by their innocent ignorance.

The decentralization of the securities business caused by the Communications Revolution will also open a new business opportunity to an entirely new group of potential stockbrokers: the regular person. This is the real democratization of the United States stockbrokerage business. The retired person, the salesman on the road, the accountant, and the teacher can all be stockbrokers today. Yes, what this decentralization creates is an opportunity for something new in the securities business. A new marketplace niche in the securities business that I will refer to as the "Part-Time Stockbroker."

A part-time stockbroker can be doing other things with his or her life than just sitting around a stockbrokerage office watching a quote machine. The stockbrokerage business can be a part-time business. Retired to Costa Rica, great! In your spare time, you can serve other retirees' investment needs and earn more than when you were working as an engineer. This transforms the stockbroker profession into a new dimension of flexibility that is still unimaginable by most people in the securities industry.

Example: A cross-country independent truck driver can be a part-time stockbroker. This man owns his own truck and works hard for his money as a truck driver. He has brains and decides to become a part-time stockbroker. He drives his rig every day and develops his clientele at truck stops. Every day at each truck stop, our truck driver is the only stockbroker there. The other independent truckers at these truck stops are, like everyone, concerned about their retirement savings and their financial future. This truck driving, part-time stockbroker can address the personal financial situation of each of these truckers. He especially understands their personal needs since he, too, is a truck driver.

Every time our truck driver stops for breakfast, lunch, or dinner, it becomes a mini-seminar to 5 or 6 other truckers who want to learn more about their own personal finances and what investment opportunities are available to them. These truckers have the need for financial services, but never had the opportunity to learn. They never had the opportunity to learn because they must work long hours and most stockbrokers would be closed when the trucker's day was over. Or even a more important reality, the truckers, out of their own personal fear of talking to a "blue blood" stockbroker about the mystical world of finance, were afraid to ask questions about their financial future. These kings of the road were intimidated by their situation. Now, they have one of their own to educate them and help serve their investment needs.

Do not worry about reaching your truck driving, part-time stockbroker. He has a cellular phone with call waiting and a beeper and a radio fax in his truck. Yes, this is just one of hundreds of examples of what I see as the revolution within the stockbrokerage business over the next 30 years. A democratization of Wall Street brought about because of decentralization. As the Communications Revolution allows massive decentralization, it will create a huge new niche in the securities business called the part-time stockbroker.

This area of the future of the stockbrokerage business is so exciting to me that I have dedicated all of Chapter Eight to this subject.

An important sidenote that I want to emphasize here is that this decentralization of the stockbrokerage business and the creation of part-time stockbrokers will create greater personal relationships between the stockbroker and the investing customer. This means that the closer the relationship between the stockbroker and the customer, the better quality of investment the securities business will provide the customer.

The Penny Stock Frauds of the 1980's were conducted by people calling strangers over the telephone and high pressuring them into a bad investment. If you have a personal relationship with someone, if you are looking them in the eye and you realize the effects of your advice and the financial needs of your clients, I believe that you, the stockbroker, will do a better job for the investor. As my 25 years of experience in the securities world has shown me, without a doubt, stockbrokers who have personal relationships with their clients do a better job for them.

3.   Lifestyle of the Changing Stockbrokerage Business

I believe more than anything that the biggest change in the future of the stockbrokerage business over the next 30 years will be due to the lifestyle changes that are occurring. These lifestyle changes are occurring because of all of the before mentioned trends and technological changes. The lifestyle changes that I foresee are comprised of desires and demands.

First, the list of desires in the lifestyle changes that are going to affect stockbrokers:

Trust: Everyone wants trust in their financial dealings. We want a relationship that allows us to trust the people that we are dealing with. We want to be comfortable with our investments. This desire for trust in our financial dealings lifestyle has always been present. This desire for trust exists now more than ever due to the savings and loan crisis and other scandals. Lincoln Savings and Loan has became an example of a pure violation of trust to every investor. Elderly retirees were sold, by cold-hearted sales people (with whom they had no personal relationship), on transferring their life savings into a faulty house of cards. We all desire trust in our financial dealings. This is a major lifestyle change occurring among all investors. Fast, cheap, and impersonal dealings in our personal finances are just not acceptable anymore.

Enlightenment and Education: Everyone now wants to know what is going on and why. Investors want trusted advisors. They also want to intellectually understand investing. We need to educate and enlighten people today and into the future.

Understanding: People want to understand things in the simple, basic truths. Today, people are suspicious of things that are complicated. People have learned over the years that when something was presented to them as complicated and they did not understand, they usually got had. If people cannot see the simple truth in something, they will avoid it.

These desires are not shocking to the reader, but obvious. These desires by investors will affect and change the way the stockbrokerage business performs in the future.

Next, are the demands in our lifestyle that will affect the stockbrokerage business:

> <u>Accountability</u>: Today and tomorrow, we are all demanding accountability for both our investments and the actions of those whom we entrust with our money. We demand that our financial representatives be held accountable for their deeds and their performance. No longer do investors have apathy in acceptance of poor results. The lifestyle has changed now so that everyone feels they have the right to hold others accountable.

All of these lifestyle changes that I see occurring in the stockbrokerage business are for the better. A lifestyle in the consumer of financial services who demand that their stockbrokers must warrant the consumer's trust and that the stockbroker must perform effectively for his or her clients. Just being a good salesman is no longer good enough for investors. Investors have grown wiser and more cautious and their lifestyle has changed. Stockbrokers can now be held accountable and today's customers are going to keep it that way.

All investors want to deal in a human personal relationship with someone, someone they can hold accountable. We all need to feel comfortable that we can trust the people we deal with. This is the lifestyle change of the future of the stockbrokerage business.

The subject of trust may seem very esoteric to many readers as it is not tangible. It is, however, very material to the future of the stockbrokerage business into the 21st Century. The lifestyle change of Americans becoming health conscious was not a tangible event. It has however changed many industries forever. Production of eggs, meat, whiskey, and cigarettes will never be the same because Americans became health conscious. New businesses sprouted up from these lifestyle changes of becoming more health conscious such as running shoes, light foods, and spring waters. These new business have boomed. The change in lifestyles within the stockbrokerage business will be almost as big as the shift caused by the lifestyle changes that occurred in people's physical health. Pay attention to the trend, it is real!

In this chapter, I have talked about the revolution within the stockbrokerage industry. There is one more component that is a part of all of the above: the investing customer of today and tomorrow. Today, the investing customer is much more educated, aware, and enlightened than only 25 years ago. In the next 30 years, the investing customer will become extremely well-informed compared to today's investors.

Hundreds of books and a passion to learn have made it possible to become an informed investor today. There is no doubt that today's investors are more analytical, more computer knowledgeable, well read, and informed than any group of investors ever before in the history of commerce. Smart customers demand that stockbrokers provide better services to them. This is now becoming a major factor in the Stockbrokers Revolution of the 21st Century.

Today, when you go into a book store, generally the largest category of books are health books. After health books, the next largest category are financial health books, as I call them, books on how to take care of your own personal financial wealth. The future of the stockbrokerage business rests with the financial health of its customers, customers who are today more assertive and more enlightened than anyone ever before. This is good news for the stockbrokerage industry overall. It is bad news for those firms that long for the old days of sheepish customers, no customer accountability, and high pressure sales tactics.

To conclude this chapter, I believe that the stockbrokerage businesses are going to overwhelm their competitors in the Financial Services Business – the banks and others. I believe part of the reason for their success will be the revolution occurring within the securities business itself. This revolution includes the ethnic marketplace being aggressively serviced by ethnic stockbrokers taking fearful savings dollars into better investment opportunities. The decentralization of the financial markets will also create a new area of the securities business, the part-time stockbrokers. These part-time stockbrokers will reach into personal investment market niches unimaginable only 10 years ago. All of this leads to greater personalization of the stockbrokerage business, thereby lessening fraud and improving investment performance. All of this leads to a lifestyle change that improves the financial health of the investor and the world.

Stockbrokers in the 21st Century will be very different from their counterparts of the 1900's. Travel, communications, computers, educational videos, and more will take the stockbrokerage industry out of the Industrial Revolution and into the Star Trek Revolution.

By the year 2020, I can hear it now, "Scottie, I am on the 14th green, beam me up 2000 shares of Philippine Long Distance Telephone. Pay for it with my German Deutch marks in my 401-K account. Then confirm all of that with our office in Bombay so Mr. Pattel knows what I am doing."

That is the 21st Century Stockbroker. That is tomorrow and it is already here today, so image how understated my vision will really be. The stockbrokerage business is the greatest business in the world and it is just getting started to enter its greatest growth phase ever.

7

THE STOCKBROKERAGE
BUSINESS OF THE 21ST CENTURY

I have already confessed that what I envision for the 21st Century Stockbroker is just an extension of what I see today. No great revelations of new technology, just the technologies that we have already implemented further into our society. I recognize that, at the rate of change occurring in technology and the world today, I am going to miss the real reality of the 21st Century Stockbroker by a very wide margin. Even knowing this, I believe for the reader it is worth the effort to explore the extensions of what I see for the stockbrokerage business of the 21st Century. Of course, I will err greatly by underestimating the changes that lie ahead.

Some of these areas will be repeats of what I have covered earlier in this book as new marketplace niches. Earlier in this book, the perspective that I took was here is a new niche in the securities marketplace that will be developed. The perspective in this chapter of the book is what the stockbrokerage business will look like in the year 2023. Our point of view in this chapter is 30 years into the future, so some of those earlier marketplace niches will by then be reality.

THE STANDARD SECURITIES BUSINESS

The standard securities business can generally be divided into 4 parts:

1. Retail Securities
2. Institutional Securities
3. Wholesale Securities
4. International Securities

Each of these areas of the securities business will evolve differently into the 21st Century. The place to start this analysis is the retail securities business. The basic reason for that being that all securities business originates (one way or another) from the retail securities business. Dealing with an individual customer is the foundation stone of the securities business. Most financial institutions are just the commingling of many individuals' investment funds.

THE RETAIL SECURITIES BUSINESS

To look at the next 30 years of the retail securities business, it is best divided into 3 parts:

Part 1: The Standard Wall Street Wire House
Part 2: The Discounters
Part 3: The Others

This will allow for logical analysis.

PART 1: THE STANDARD RETAIL WALL STREET WIRE HOUSE

The standard Wall Street wire house will remain pretty much the same as today. The major securities wire houses have a good business and adjust to all the basic marketplace changes fairly well. The Wall Street wire houses will maintain their basic business philosophy and operations. These wire houses implement technology very well and stay attuned to their customers.

Of the new niche markets developing within the securities industry that I have described, I do not believe that the major Wall Street wire houses will respond to or develop any of them for themselves. They will ignore these new marketplace niches in the securities business the same as they ignored the discount stockbrokerage business opportunity before by not openly responding to the competition of the discount stockbrokers when the discounters started in competition with the wire houses' basic business in the 1970's and 1980's. The major Wall Street firms realized that they had more business to lose than they had to gain by attacking their own primary business franchise.

The greatest future problem area for the major Wall Street wire houses is that the same sales strength that made them so powerful in the securities business is now under assault. The new lifestyle of investor disapproves of "cold calling." The new lifestyle of investor disapproves of being sold something. This is an area that the major firms are aware of and are working on. Yet, the major firms have not sensed the change in lifestyle that is starting to alienate their style of business from the evolving customers.

Into the 21st Century, the standard stockbrokerage Wall Street wire house will remain competitive. However, their share of the overall marketplace in the stockbrokerage business will be reduced, in my opinion, by half of what it is today. An analogy of the situation would be that the major wire houses are the Sears of the stockbrokerage business, still a competitor, but not what they used to be.

PART 2: THE DISCOUNT STOCKBROKERAGE FIRMS

These members of the stockbrokerage business have become the technological innovators of the securities business. Home computer access, 24 hour trading, and this and that, bells and whistles have made them awesome competitors. Like Price Club or any other discounter, their business is based upon price and impersonal service.

The discount stockbrokers are going to command a large market share of the stockbrokerage business in the 21st Century. Yet, I do not see that market share being much larger than it is already today. From my exposure, I see many people leaving the discount stockbrokers because they want a more personal relationship. For example, medical clinics are cheaper than private doctors' office visits, yet many people prefer to pay the difference in price for the greater personal comfort of a private physician. Similarly, many investors are learning that cheap is not always better.

The discount stockbrokerage firms will remain technological leaders in the 21st Century stockbrokerage industry. Yet, their market share will not grow as their customers struggle between two major trends: one, educated and enlightened investors (a plus for the discount stockbrokers), and two, the desire for personalized relationships with their financial advisor (a negative for discounters).

There will be discounters in 2020. Those that have a more personal relationship with their customers will be doing better than those that merely offer inexpensive rates.

PART 3: OTHERS IN THE STOCKBROKERAGE BUSINESS

This is the area where I see the most growth in market share into the 21st Century. This area will be divided up between financial planners and part-time stockbrokers.

I believe the retail stockbrokerage business in the future will develop another major marketplace niche. This will be similar to what happened with the securities marketplace with the creation of the discount stockbrokers.

In the overall spectrum of the securities business, stockbroker discount firms are perceived low cost and low service. Wall Street wire houses are perceived as standard cost with higher services. With this general mindset, I believe there is a new marketplace niche in the securities business: very high levels of personalized service for standard cost.

People will pay the standard price for high quality service. For example, if you have Price Club at one end of the marketplace spectrum (the discounter) and Sears in the middle of the marketplace spectrum (standard department store), there is a need for a Nordstrom in the marketplace with higher personal service at standard prices.

Stockbrokers who can educate and provide very high levels of personal service will show investors that, when it comes to investing, the highest cost of investing is not the commission paid to a full service stockbroker. The highest cost to the investor is the Interest Rate Spread the investor left at the bank in regard to investment returns. Personalized stockbrokers will demonstrate to investors that the highest cost of investing is ignorance not commissions.

Yes, as more and more people learn about the advantages of securities investing, they will prefer someone they know and trust. For teaching them about finance, people will desire someone who is not impersonal and cheap. Financial planners and part-time stockbrokers are the two major benefactors of the future changes in the Financial Services Business.

After that brief analysis of the future of the stockbrokerage business, I now want to expand upon 2 areas of the retail securities business I perceive as very fast growing over the next 30 years.

The retail securities business over the next 30 years will grow most dynamically in 2 non-traditional niches:

1.   The International Opportunity
2.   Part-Time Stockbrokers

THE INTERNATIONAL OPPORTUNITY

In most nations of the world, the concept of a retail securities distribution system is unheard of. Only the United States, Canada, and Japan have developed retail securities markets distribution systems. After those 3 nations, the retail securities distribution scale drops to another league which includes Britain, Hong Kong, Singapore, India, and other former British Colonies. Then, after those nations, you drop a long way down to the other European nations which, in many ways, are just barely ahead of the underdeveloped nations with laws. The next lowest group of nations are the underdeveloped nations that have the legal, accounting, and banking systems in place (generally from historical basis), but no real securities market. The last group of nations on the scale are the former Communist nations that do not even have the laws in place to allow securities business.

Over the next 10 years, I believe we are going to see an amazing development of the retail securities business in countries outside the United States. The first area to develop their retail securities business will be Europe. Following Europe, there will be Asia, then Latin America, and last, Africa.

It is important to note that where you have the most developed capital markets in the world, you have the wealthiest populations. Where you have the weakest capital markets, you have the poorest populations. Coincidence? No! It is the result of Free Market Economics. No capital means no commerce, no commerce means no wealth creation, no wealth creation means poverty.

Many people complain about the concept of Free Market Economics and the creation of trickle down economic growth and wealth. These people should see the poverty that a drought of trickle down causes. Capital is like the rain: where it falls, things grow, where it does not fall, nothing grows, all you have is poverty.

Which comes first, capital markets or a wealthy population? That's easy, the capital markets must come first. No capital markets, no economic development. It is always a shock to me how a nation supposedly opens up its economy for development and declares it now wants international investors, but then keeps its national capital markets closed or antiquated.

Capital market development is the first step towards developing a nation. The first step towards creating a domestic capital market is the creation of retail stockbrokers in that nation and a securities distribution system. This is the reason I see tremendous growth for the retail stockbrokerage business internationally over the next 30 years. In the 21st Century, you will see the rapid and sophisticated expansion of the retail securities business in many nations around the world.

The great financial names of the past decades, such as the Rothschilds, Hopes, and Morgans, have become overshadowed and replaced by the modern day American and Japanese financial firms that have created a retail securities distribution systems: Merrill Lynch, Shearson, Dean Witter, Paine Webber, Nomura, and others. If you want to know who is going to be the great wealth in Russia, Nigeria, Mexico, or the Philippines in the 21st Century, just look at who is building a retail securities distribution system today in those countries.

The International Development of Retail Securities Business will be a tremendous and rewarding program.

THE PART-TIME STOCKBROKER

This area will be covered specifically in Chapter Eight of this book. However, I want to introduce it here in this context to the reader. The second major area of business opportunity for the retail stockbrokerage business is the part-time stockbroker.

I see this area of the stockbrokerage business as a tremendous marketplace opportunity within the United States and Europe now. There is huge opportunity in these two great marketplaces today. A few others, like the Philippines, are also ready for the concept of the part-time stockbroker. Where you have a well educated population and static commercial banks, the opportunities are great.

A nation that has many members of the population capable of providing basic investor services is sitting in a position to advance into this marketplace easily. That would include all the basic investment steps such as financial planning, analysis, tax planning, portfolio strategies, and execution. Areas of specialized investment expertise are rarely utilized by most stockbrokers to service their clients. Most New York wire houses would not let their average stockbroker deal in these areas anyway, such as Corporate Finance, Trading, Research, Institutional Business, and such areas are outside the realm of most traditional stockbrokers anyway.

So, if it's a given that 90% of the securities business is the basics, what keeps an accountant, an engineer, a teacher, or a retired person from learning the basics of investing and then serving clients on a very personalized basis? Nothing! This is the basis of the part-time stockbroker.

I see a major growth in the area of retail securities business expanding into a part-time profession for those who have the desire and aptitude for handling financial basics.

I see accountants becoming part-time stockbrokers. Why, if there were a choice, would an accountant work to develop a client base, incurring all the hard detailed accounting work, and then refer the client to a hot shot stockbroker? The stockbroker keeps the commission from any investments the client makes and then, if the stockbroker hurts the client, the stockbroker sends him back to the accountant, broke and angry.

Why wouldn't a high school teacher learn the basics about becoming a stockbroker and then assist the 60 other teachers on the faculty at her school? Why wouldn't a sales manager for an electronics company build-up a clientele of select customers to help them invest wisely? What real estate broker would not be dually licensed so that he could handle both securities and real estate investments? What retiree would not want to earn a few extra thousand dollars per month by helping other retirees invest wisely? For example, I met a man who was getting ready to retire from his position of Chief Financial Officer of a major corporation. This man became a part-time stockbroker so he could help other retirees and make a few extra dollars. This man was more capable than 90% of the stockbrokers I have ever met.

Earlier in this book, I talked about relationship stockbrokers. The entire concept of a part-time stockbroker is directed at a very personal relationship as it relates to the securities business. The part-time stockbroker already has a working relationship with the investors in another capacity, that of their full-time or other part-time job or situation. The part-time stockbroker's intelligence and character are already a known quality to their potential clients, all that is needed are investment products.

I see the next major development in the retail securities business will be the part-time stockbroker. The ability of the part-time stockbroker to capture the highly personal investment relationship business and to be stockbrokers in every nook and cranny in America is almost mind boggling.

Just as the stockbrokerage discounters arrived and captured their piece of the securities marketplace, I see the part-time stockbrokers doing the same. They will be capturing relationship driven business through an extension of their present business and social relationships, and will be able to service that business through the utilization of technology. This will bring investing clients better service than any standard stockbroker can today.

SUMMATION OF THE 21ST CENTURY RETAIL STOCKBROKERAGE BUSINESS

The Wall Street wire houses and the discounters will continue to prosper. The major growth areas will be the others in the stockbrokerage business, the financial planners and the new area of part-time stockbrokers.

INSTITUTIONAL MARKETPLACES FOR STOCKBROKERS IN THE 21ST CENTURY

The institutional marketplace for the 21st Century is easy to foresee, it is already there. The United States institutional stockbrokers are the world's most advanced and awesome. I cannot even speculate on how they can improve upon what is, in my opinion, already in the 21st Century and beyond my comprehension.

I believe one of the secrets to success in the general retail securities business is to study what the institutional stockbrokers are implementing and then attempt to apply it to the retail securities business.

There is nothing that I can add to this area of the stockbrokerage business.

THE WHOLESALE STOCKBROKERAGE BUSINESS INTO THE 21ST CENTURY

This is one of my favorite areas of the securities business. It really does not have a place in this book since it only exists in the United States. The wholesale stockbrokerage business is extremely sophisticated and one of my personal pet projects. Securities wholesalers in the United States today are ultra-sophisticated, they are already into the Star Trek mentality when it comes to their business.

Securities wholesalers will not change much over the next 30 years into the 21st Century and their business will remain very profitable as always. Where the growth and profits will come from is the introduction of wholesale securities into international markets and across international borders. This will be big business!

THE INTERNATIONAL SECURITIES BUSINESS

The traditional international securities business will become a blending of all of the segments discussed above. Presently, 90% of all international securities business is done between major financial institutions. By the year 2020, institutions will be less than half of the international securities business as individuals expand their reach and search for better investments.

United States stockbrokerage firms will develop the retail securities distribution systems in the international securities marketplaces. United States stockbrokers will develop the wholesaling marketplace of the international securities business and the growth there will be phenomenal.

Keep this thought in mind about the development of the international securities business over the next 30 years: RETIREMENT!

Think I have gone crazy.

Millions of people upon reaching retirement age are migrating to a less expensive place to retire. One million, five hundred thousand British citizens have retired to Spain. Over 300,000 United States citizens have retired in Costa Rica, and more than that in Mexico. To retire in Japan, a person needs $3,000 per month to survive. That $3,000 per month means the person will be forced to live like a prisoner: cramped living space, no leisure facilities, and no joy. For $1,000 per month, that same person could retire to the Philippines and live like a king: servants, a mansion, golfing, fishing, and more.

The Baby Boomers in the United States are more international than their parents. The Baby Boomers will also need to stretch their retirement funds farther if they are going to last. The developing world is naturally very beautiful. With some of today's technologies, you could develop a retirement paradise in Argentina, Africa, Philippines, Turkey, Mexico, and Panama to mention a few. Warm weather, beautiful beaches, low medical cost, low food cost, and all of the modern conveniences does not sound bad.

By the year 2030, I predict that 30,000,000 American citizens will retire outside of the United States. The biggest reverse migration in the history of mankind.

The citizens of the poor countries are migrating to the United States to get high paying jobs. Retirees of the United States are migrating to poor countries to live less expensively, better, and longer.

So as this huge migration of wealthy and semi-wealthy Americans migrates into the developing world, you will see the creation of the securities business systems to follow them. Where go the customers, so go I.

SUMMATION OF THE STOCKBROKERAGE BUSINESS IN THE 21ST CENTURY

I can summarize the stockbrokerage business in the 21st Century as the convergence of all the macro trends of communications, computers, internationalization, lifestyle, and economic reality. The stockbrokerage business is extremely dynamic. I know it will supersede my humble abilities to forecast its destiny over the next 30 years. What I do know is that it is the greatest business in the world and getting even better for at least the next 30 years.

8

PART-TIME STOCKBROKERS AND THEIR FUTURE IN THE 21ST CENTURY

This book is about the future of the stockbrokerage business. A new marketplace niche within the stockbrokerage business, that I believe will develop, will be the area of the part-time stockbroker. Because I believe the part-time stockbroker will be a major new segment of the stockbrokerage business in the 21st Century, I wanted to go into greater depth for the reader about this new and exciting area of the business. I believe that the flexibility of technology, communications, and our lifestyles will change the way stockbrokers interact with their customers today and especially tomorrow. I want to expand on this area of the future for the securities business because, for you the reader, it could open up a whole new world of possibilities.

Before I go into why I believe part-time stockbrokers will be a new segment in the stockbrokerage business, I want to explain why individuals will <u>want</u> to become part-time stockbrokers.

My experience in this area divides people who want to become part-time stockbrokers into 4 basic categories:

1. Future Full-time Career
2. Supplement Income
3. Personalized Investing
4. Greater Knowledge

FUTURE FULL-TIME CAREER

The category of a future full-time stockbroker is the easiest category to explain. A person wants to become a stockbroker. He or she wants to earn the average reported income of $114,000 or better per year for stockbrokers. This person who wants to be a full-time stockbroker is, at this time, not in a personal financial situation to become a full-time stockbroker. He or she cannot transition into the securities business without clients or an assured monthly income and, for that matter, without much experience in the investment business.

This person decides to becomes a part-time stockbroker for now. Then, slowly and deliberately over time, he or she starts to build an investing clientele and some investing experience. With some time and experience, this person builds up a clientele and a dependable monthly income stream. At that time, the person can transition into a full-time stockbroker position.

So category one is people who are preparing to become a full-time stockbroker. They are pursuing that objective a little at a time to make the transition smoother.

SUPPLEMENTAL INCOME

The second category is comprised of those people who want to supplement their monthly income. These are generally people who are very happy in their present career and their objective is just that they want to supplement their monthly income.

Examples of this type of person are teachers or Government workers. They want to keep their present job, but want to earn extra money using their brains and helping their fellow workers or associates. A teacher having a personal relationship with the members of the school faculty can service their retirement needs. It is better for the investor clients to have a friendly and informative stockbroker close at hand. The teacher as a part-time stockbroker could earn an extra $1,000 - $15,000 per month.

A part-time stockbroker may only earn an extra $3,000 per month. By full-time stockbroker standards, that would be a very low monthly income. Yet, to a school teacher who is presently earning only $36,000 per year, it is a material increase in monthly take-home pay. So people want to supplement their present monthly income can become part-time stockbrokers.

PERSONALIZED INVESTING

The third area is comprised of people who are interested in personal investing. These individuals want to have a very limited clientele and service them on a very personalized basis. An example of this would be a retired person who wants to service a small group of people who need someone of his quality and training. This person does not want to be burdened with a lot of responsibilities. In this category, I have seen medical doctors that served themselves and perhaps five fellow doctors.

Retirees are a major component of this category. These people are the type of people who like investing and want to be able to help others invest intelligently, but want to do it on a limited basis.

GREATER KNOWLEDGE

The fourth category is comprised of those people that become stockbrokers for greater knowledge. These are individuals who for some reason know they are going to be involved with the Financial Services Business in their future and want to know more about it. This includes individuals anticipating retirement, inheritance, or future funding of their ventures.

Also included in this category are people who want to know what the real story is behind discount commissions. Is it true that No Load Mutual Funds can cost the investors more than Load Funds? Is it true that discount commission stockbrokers can be more expensive than full service stockbrokers? All of this is important to these people and they want to know the real world as a stockbroker knows investing.

These four reasons are the primary reasons a person would consider becoming a part-time stockbroker. Now we can discuss the reason I see the part-time stockbroker as a major growth area in the Financial Services Industry in the 21st Century.

THE PRIME DIRECTIVE

The primary issue about being a stockbroker is, what does it take to be a stockbroker? In plain words, what is the prime directive of a stockbroker?

I can summarize the prime directive of a stockbroker in one short sentence, "Doing what is best for the customer." In the 25 years that I have been a stockbroker, I have learned that computer research, trading access, and everything else is meaningless unless the stockbroker does what is best for the client. This may mean the client needs higher and safer income by owning triple A corporate bonds. If the stockbroker is brilliant, but the client is lost, confused, and scared, then the relationship is not good for the client. Too often I have seen where the stockbroker thought he was brilliant and went ahead and did what he wanted for the client (the end justifies the means syndrome), only to wipe out the client with excessive trading or unsuitable investments. The primary task of a good stockbroker, unquestionable in my mind, is doing what is best for the client.

What then are the qualifications to do what is best for the client? The first thing is obvious: "Know the client's needs and wants." What are the abilities of the client (psychologically and economically)? Once the stockbroker understands the client and his or her personal situation, then and only then can the stockbroker take care of the customer's needs.

When I was a young man chasing high returns through high technology investing, I refused to deal with anyone who did not have their basic investment situation already in place since I only handled risk capital investments. I wanted assurances (often in writing) that a person's personal finances were established and that the money we were using was their risk money. At that time, I wanted nothing to do with bonds or preferred stocks. Nothing distracted me from my primary investment pursuit to know which high tech company was going to be the next big winner.

Well, that was when I was 22 years old. I knew I was going to succeed, so I did not worry about tomorrow. I knew that tomorrow would always be better for me and my family. As the years have passed and I made money, I started to learn that I needed savings and retirement savings.

I started saving, utilizing bonds, dividend stocks, and other programs to invest. I found that I no longer worried about how to get rich, but how to stay rich. The same economic lifecycle of phases has even happened to me.

Some of my friends who were hot shots, like me, have died. They were successful and young, yet they died and their families were faced with more difficult financial problems than how to get richer. Their real problem was how to survive on the money left after the death of my friends. Now, I find myself not concerned with which new company might make us a fortune, but how do I help my friends' families prepare for paying for college in 10 years? How do my friends' wives face the next 40 years without their husbands or the income they had always anticipated?

I have learned a lot from these experiences, but the most important thing I learned was that a stockbroker has to know and understand what the circumstances of the customer are, not what the stockbroker wants to sell a customer. It is that issue alone, doing what is right for the customer, that makes me love the relationship area of the securities business versus the transaction side of the business.

Historically, the stockbrokerage business was a very relationship driven business. Then, with deregulation in 1975, the business changed. Discounting commissions and cold calling caused the business to degenerate into cheaper and cheaper executions and the selling of false dreams to susceptible people.

The centralization of the securities business at that time, attempting to service the decentralized population, caused greater and greater distances between the stockbrokers and their customers. This has lead to major problems: The lessening of quality of investment products and the lack of care some stockbrokers have for their customers. All of this has rattled the stockbrokerage business.

For example, look at the lawsuits and arbitration proceedings within the securities business today. It scares customers, stockbrokers, and stockbrokerage firms. A return to the personal relationship of investing is needed and wanted. That is part of the future I see for the 21st Century Stockbroker and this is why I believe so strongly in the future of the part-time stockbroker. If caring about the client's needs and wants is the primary requirement towards success as a stockbroker, then many people can qualify in that regard.

Since I am the self-proclaimed spokesman for the part-time stockbroker concept, I believe that I need to answer a question in the reader's mind here, even before you ask it. The most common question that I get about the concept of part-time stockbrokers is, "How can they do a job as well as a full-time stockbroker?" That is easy to answer since I believe the primary purpose of a good stockbroker is servicing the investment needs and wants of the clients. I see that the answer rests solely upon the nature of the stockbroker, full or part-time. I don't see why someone who has another job or profession does not have the ability to be caring for the client's best interest. In fact, from my experience, I see the opposite.

Too often in my life as a stockbroker, I have seen full-time stockbrokers sell something that was wrong for the customer because the stockbroker needed to earn commissions. In my experience with part-time stockbrokers, they are all noticeably more concerned about the customer's needs and wants and less concerned about generating commissions. Since the commissions are extra income for doing a good job, part-time stockbrokers do not pressure customers into bad investments or churn accounts.

Also, I have noticed that part-time stockbrokers generally place their customers' needs much higher than they place their own needs for commissions. If the primary standard for the measure of a stockbroker is that they do what is best for the client, then there is no doubt that it is the <u>nature</u> of the person that counts and not the amount of hours they put in at the office.

Part-time stockbrokers, I believe, will become a large and very vibrant part of the future of the securities business. Real world experience demonstrates that a person with knowledge and caring can do a terrific job for his or her investor clients. Part-time stockbrokers can put in whatever hours they wish and still be very good stockbrokers for their customers. Doing what is right for the customers is what matters as far as being a good stockbroker. Wise, caring, and experienced part-time stockbrokers working two hours a week are better for the investing clients than a young, full-time stockbroker who is in the office selling index options on the phone to little old ladies in retirement.

EXAMPLES OF PART-TIME STOCKBROKERS

Now I want to provide some very simple examples of the type of people I see becoming part-time stockbrokers in the future. These very specific situations and examples will be used just to open the imagination of the reader. There are hundreds of other possibilities and examples that could be used. With this small sampling, I will miss many possibilities. Yet, these examples will allow the intelligent reader to expand and extrapolate the concepts of the part-time stockbroker. This will help you see the massive business opportunities present for the securities business. You, the reader, will be able to envision possibilities that I cannot imagine. The primary examples of part-time stockbrokers that I will focus upon are:

1. A Retired Person
2. An Accountant

3. A Business Person
4. A Teacher
5. An Engineer
6. A Police or Fire Person
7. A Real Estate or Mortgage Broker
8. An Insurance Agent

This small sample of examples of part-time stockbrokers will provide the reader the flavor of the concept of part-time stockbrokers. This new concept of the part-time stockbroker, I believe, will revolutionize the stockbrokerage business more than the concept of the discount brokerage business has affected the securities business.

Remember, I have a very strong premise in my calculations, I believe money is too important to the average person to be treated coldly and uncaringly. I believe that a person's money is very personal and that the stockbroker working with the client should do what is best for the client, not what is best for the broker.

To accomplish that objective, the stockbroker needs to know the customer's needs, wants, and capacity for uncertainty and worry. To truly understand that person's situation, I believe that life's experiences help. I believe that a 70 year old retired women who has to live off of a fixed income is more capable of understanding the fears and needs of another 70 year old retired woman. Yes, much more than a 22 year old, fresh college graduate who wants to make his fortune before he is 30. I believe that human interface and caring is more important than brilliance. I know that if that 70 year old retired lady, who is a part-time stockbroker, personally understands her clients' situation, she can take better care of them.

There will sometimes arise a specific ultra-sophisticated investment need that develops every now and then for a client. However, when that occurs, a telephone call to the Estate Tax Specialist, or any other specialist within the stockbrokerage firm, can be made to support the part-time stockbroker. An example of an extraordinary need would be a question of estate taxation verses gift taxes for estate planning. Just because a stockbrokerage firm has an Estate Tax Specialist working for them full-time does not mean that the specialist is good with clients or truly understands their needs. If that specialist spends the entire day reading tax books, the specialist will undoubtedly be great with taxes, but probably lousy with humans.

I believe the future of part-time stockbrokers is having a real human and personal relationship with the investing customer. Then by calling the tax specialist, they can work together to better serve the client on business that is other than basic. The most important part of the stockbroker's business, as far as I am concerned, is to know the client. Then call upon the specialist available if a unique special situation arises. So, in each of the examples I am providing, the primary focus is upon the task of having or developing a personal relationship with the clients. Once the stockbroker knows the client's needs and nature, then specialists can be brought in to assist if needed.

RETIREES

The one area where we will see many part-time stockbrokers is the retirees marketplace. Millions of intelligent and experienced people with a lifetime of experience are retiring every year. These people are still very capable of being part-time stockbrokers. All they need to do to build up a clientele is to serve the needs of other retirees.

The area where I see the real development of retiree part-time stockbrokers is among today's 55 year olds and the future Baby Boomers. A 55 year old person today who looks into the future and says, "I can keep my job at ABC Company until I retire in 10 years. I can study and become a part-time stockbroker now and, when I retire, I will have another source of income." That person will then be in a position to continue working for ABC Company until his retirement. Upon retirement, he can act as a part-time stockbroker just serving the needs of other retirees. He can serve the retirees that are looking for a close personal relationship with someone they know and trust.

I met a 67 year old lady who was a part-time stockbroker. She told me that she had decided to become a stockbroker after she had lost a lot of money in the stock market. This woman lost her money because of a young stockbroker with a lot of hot ideas and lousy performance. She decided from that experience that she and her friends needed a stockbroker understood their special needs as retirees. From that start, this woman built a great clientele of retired customers on one statement, "I will not let anyone hurt you." She told me that all of her clientele were retirees and that all of the retirees she met wanted a stockbroker who was in their similar circumstances. These retired investors all wanted someone who understood that they could not afford to lose their principal.

I believe a major area of the future part-time stockbrokers will be the retired business person, a person with a full background of experience and knowledge. Retired people are prime examples of what

I believe will develop in the future of the 21st Century stockbrokerage business. Obviously, a person's brain does not stop working on the first day of retirement. These retired business people can become part-time stockbrokers and develop a clientele of other retirees.

Wisdom, experience, knowledge, understanding, and compassion, what more could anyone want from a stockbroker? How comfortable would a 70 year old retiree be with another person in similar circumstances of age, needs, and concerns? Very comfortable. The widow can turn to another widow who understands her situation. These women understand each other better than a sharped-tongued 23 year stockbroker out of New York City's latest high pressure sales shop, pushing a new issue of another high tech company.

Many of today's retirees have, for some reason, decided that they are either incapable of thinking effectively after age 65 or have disenfranchised themselves from using their brains and their hearts in order to help others with similar investment needs, others who are less qualified to take care of their personal financial needs and need help from a caring and concerned part-time stockbroker.

Too often, I have see very capable people retired. I have seen them ignore or fail to help protect their fellow retirees from the wolves that stalk them out of their retirement money. I believe that some retirees should become part-time stockbrokers not only so that they can earn a few extra dollars, but to help protect other retirees from the horror stories we all hear too often. Most retirees have the mental capabilities of becoming a stockbroker and serving a clientele, they have the ability to serve the special needs of the other retirees with both competency and compassion.

Now I know there is someone out their reading this book saying, "Hey, I don't want to work every day in some office as a stockbroker, that's why I retired." Let me address your concern. In the 21st Century future that I foresee, I don't expect you to come into the office except, of course, when you want to visit or for required regulator meetings. I do not envision the retired part-time broker becoming a stock jockey and being in the office by 6:30 a.m. for day trading! What I envision is that the part-time retiree stockbroker will develop a relationship with the client. They will understand the client's situation, the needs, the wants, the capacity to invest the client's money. Then the part-time stockbroker will develop the investment programs and policies that reflect that client's investment needs. Finally, utilizing the specialist at the stockbrokerage firm, carry out those investment policies and programs for the customers.

The 83 year old retiree can be the part-time stockbroker who has a client relationship with a 92 year old retiree, a person who needs safe and dependable income such as triple A corporate bonds. Once the investment programs are in place, the details of paperwork and being in the office can be handled through a joint internal stockbroker relationship. The part-time stockbroker, through the firm where he works, will set up the account with an internal stockbroker. The internal stockbroker will be responsible for the day-to-day work on the customers' accounts while the retiree part-time broker handles the relationship and the investment policies of the accounts.

Yes, I believe that the retirees of the 21st Century will become responsible for a major part of the Financial Revolution I envision. The Communications Revolution and the Lifestyle Revolution will provide them opportunities and capabilities which will let them serve the tremendous investment needs of other retirees.

The Baby Boomer generation was born from 1946 through 1966. These Baby Boomers entered their first phase of life as kiddies. They liked Mattel toys and Disney movies and, when those Baby Boomers bought from those companies, those companies prospered. Then the Baby Boomers aged and became hippies. As teenagers and hippies, they liked Volkswagens, rock and roll music, and a relaxed lifestyle. Those companies that serviced those wants and needs of the teenage Baby Boomers prospered. Then the Baby Boomers became older and they became known as Yuppies. They bought houses, white wine, and BMW's, and those industries that served them prospered.

Now, the Baby Boomers are becoming savers and investors. The stockbrokerage business will benefit from this trend today. As the Baby Boomers prepare for their retirement, they will save and invest like no other generation in the history of mankind. Yet, it is the phase after this saving phase that I believe will substantially contribute to my vision of the 21st Century Stockbroker.

This phase occurs when the Baby Boomer generation retires and becomes "Woppies." Woppies stands for Wealthy Older Persons. The retired Baby Boomers are going to be healthier, both physically and financially, than any generation ever. These Woppies are going to want medical doctors and financial doctors. That's right, financial doctors to take care of their financial health. That means stockbrokers will be in great demand by these Woppies. However, unlike previous generations of retirees, the Baby Boomers will want to serve themselves.

These Baby Boomers have lived through the Computer, Travel, Communication, and Information Revolutions. They are very different from the generations that preceded them. They will serve their own fellow retirees. With the Communications Revolution and the concept of joint sharing of customers for office support, these Woppies know that they can do a better job of caring and understanding their own generation's investment needs, they know they can do better than some 24 years old stockbroker from New York City. When I am 70, it will be the year 2022. I know I would have a difficult time trusting someone who was born in 1998 with my life's savings!

Over the next 10 years, you will see the vanguard of the generation born before the Baby Boomers (the Depression Babies) start setting the trend to become part-time stockbrokers. After them, you will see the Baby Boomers make part-time stockbrokerage happen on a very massive scale starting in 2005. The retired part-time stockbroker is a massive wave of the future. You will be able to watch it grow and swell as it develops by serving the needs of its contemporaries. The 21st Century Stockbroker will be very different.

Remember one thing about the profession of a stockbroker, it is different than any other business. Once you become a stockbroker, your securities license becomes more valuable every year of your life; every grey hair, every wrinkle, every day of life's experience makes you wiser and more knowledgeable. Life's experiences really matter in the world of finance. It is the only business that I know of which becomes more valuable with time.

Retirees will become a major category of part-time stockbrokers for the reasons that I have mentioned and I believe that the primary benefactors will be other retirees.

ACCOUNTANTS

Accountants will also become a major segment of the part-time stockbrokers concept that I foresee. Being a stockbroker is a simple extension of an accountant's present business. The accountant's present business is accounting for and managing their clients' money. The management of that money may include tax preparation or tax planning. Historically, accountants in the United States have not handled investment planning.

If accountants are keeping track of the cash flow and taxes of a business, why are they not capable of helping to make investment decisions? In Europe, accountants are automatically qualified by their professional experience as accountants to deal in securities.

The United States is one of the few countries in the world that requires accountants to be additionally licensed to deal in investment products. In most nations, accountants are considered to be quite capable of understanding business sufficiently to handle investments. I consider myself an accountant, so I find it quite humorous that in the United States accountants need to take a special examination to become stockbrokers. Yet, how many stockbrokers in the United States can understand a trial balance and what the financial statements tell is really going on financially at a company?

The 21st Century Stockbroker will see the evolution of accountants move more and more into the Financial Services Industry as providers of investment advice and execution.

There are some laws within the United States today that restrict accountants from competing in the Financial Services Industry. These laws are being repealed every day and freeing up this new area for accountants to become part-time stockbrokers. The repeal of these laws will place United States' accountants on the same level as their counterparts in Europe.

This is a new and exciting segment for the United States' stockbrokerage business that is just now getting started. The capabilities of accountants to become part-time stockbrokers as an extension of their present business is, in my mind, a given. The overall potential for the stockbrokerage business is massive.

This area of securities development will mean more professionalism for the securities business and more conservative investments for the clients. When you are doing someone's taxes every year, you know that person better than a stockbroker who is cold calling on the telephone. You are also going to be more cautious with their money since you will see them again next year.

As the accounting profession becomes more diversified and extends its business areas, you will see more and more part-time stockbrokers who are also accountants. Again, lifestyle and communication will make it happen.

BUSINESS PEOPLE

Business people as future part-time stockbrokers is a natural extension of the stockbrokerage business to me. In both the world of business and the stockbrokerage industry, personal relationships are what matters.

If a sales manager of an electronics company wants to become a stockbroker part-time, what does he need to service a few clients? Easy answer - business acumen, common sense, and the ability to execute and source data. The sales manager already has most of those! The only thing the manager lacks to be a stockbroker is a place to execute and a source of data. Both of those can be provided by a telephone/fax machine and a good internal support staff at his stockbrokerage firm.

In my 25 years in the securities business, I have spent a lot of time in the field (out of the office). Yet, my customers have not suffered in the least. I call into the office continually to follow up on investment policy decisions and the major concerns of my clients. My office staff is fully licensed and competent to handle and execute urgent matters. My staff can provide a source of data, information, and analysis for both myself and my clients.

If an investor called a full-time stockbroker at a major wire house on a certain company or special situation, that stockbroker would most likely have to call the firm's internal specialist for an update or the information. So there is no difference if the full-time stockbroker is sitting at a desk in an office in downtown New York or at a pay phone in an airport in Omaha. The data is the same, the analysis is the same, and the stockbroker still has to utilize the wisdom and experience for the client. It does not matter where a stockbroker is sitting, what does matter is the personal relationship with the client and the knowledge and caring of the stockbroker, whether full or part-time.

I envision many business people will become part-time stockbrokers in the future. Small business owners, shop owners, sales people, operations managers, and more will be 21st Century part-time stockbrokers. For people already in business, becoming a stockbroker is a simple extension of their present business acumen. It is just the extension of their business knowledge into another area of business.

As illustration, a women managing a Chinese restaurant in San Francisco can be a part-time stockbroker. From her affiliation with a quality stockbrokerage firm, she would be provided with investment ideas. She is then just as qualified to tell her customers about an investment opportunity as any 23 year old stockbroker from New York City. That New York City stockbroker will never see these people face-to-face as this woman will see her customers every week. She will care about her clients and be an excellent stockbroker.

The Communications Revolution means that anyone in business who has the desire can become a stockbroker. With a stockbrokerage firm that supports them, these business people can service their investment clients as well as anyone else in the securities business. Or maybe even better since they have a personal relationship with and more personal concern and compassion for the investor.

Several years ago, I was in what was then known as West Germany to study the Turkish guest workers and their investment patterns and potentials. A Turkish commercial bank was attempting to learn how to gather the savings of the 2.5 million Turkish guest workers in Germany. I visited most of Germany studying this situation. My conclusion was that the owners of the Turkish grocery markets were the best agents to act for the bank. These owners of the Turkish grocery markets in West Germany were sharp business people. Maybe they had no great education, but they understood money. Within one year, the grocers proved my conclusion that business people can handle money and make good investment advice. I know that this is not a surprising revelation to the reader.

Business people as part-time stockbrokers is a New Wave of development of the Financial Services Business into the 21st Century.

TEACHERS

Today, hundreds of thousands of teachers throughout the United States are facing lay-offs or pay reductions. This provides a dismal future for highly educated teachers as the entire area of education is being restructured within our society. I have seen teachers who have become stockbrokers part-time and then just served the needs of the faculty at their school. I have seen these teachers as part-time stockbrokers earn an extra $3,000 to $5,000 per month. While by normal stockbrokerage monthly income standards that is very low, for a teacher who is only earning $3,000 to $4,000 per month salary, it is a significant addition to his or her monthly income. Also, the other teachers at the school are much better served than they would have been by a stranger.

The secret to financial success in the stockbrokerage business is knowledge. Teachers have the ability to learn and educate others about their financial needs and the investment products available to satisfy those needs. Educating investors as to what their investment needs are is what most stockbrokers will have to do to succeed in the 21st Century. A teacher should be able to do that easily. Teachers are a major area of future growth of part-time stockbrokers as they already have almost all of the qualifications.

ENGINEERS

Engineers are a major growth area for stockbrokers. In southern California, we have seen many people from the Defense and Aerospace Industry become stockbrokers, both full-time and part-time. The Aerospace Industry engineers are what come to my mind when I think of the engineering profession. Yet, I am sure that what is true here for Aerospace Engineers applies to all other fields of engineering as well.

Massive lay-offs in the Aerospace Industry mean that extremely educated and intelligent people are being put out on the streets where the future is bleak. How many jobs will these educated, intelligent people find designing laser inactive stabilizers for a project to Venus? Not many. Those types of jobs are just not the type of assignments that occur every day. These highly qualified people are feeling the blunt effect of this nation's transition from a war-time economy to a peace-time economy. Where are these people to go and what are they to do?

Some are becoming part-time stockbrokers while they still have an aerospace job. While working part-time as stockbrokers, they start building a clientele. When the industry lay-offs occur, the aerospace engineers easily shift to become full-time stockbrokers because they have already acquired their securities license and established their client base. If lay-offs do not occur, the engineers still have a nice part-time income and great investment experience.

I know of a gentleman who was an aerospace engineer who was laid off from his company and utilized his part-time stockbrokerage business foundation to go full-time. This man then built an excellent stockbrokerage clientele by servicing other aerospace people who were also getting laid off. He built his business by giving seminars on how to prepare for the lay-off, concerning topics such as what to do with the 401-K and what to do about health insurance.

Some of the greatest minds of our nation are being put out on the streets. People who thought of how to make this country the greatest military might in the world can easily serve investors' needs. From retirement planning to high tech investment selection, these engineers are capable of handling the business.

Not every engineer can become a stockbroker. Only a small portion will become stockbrokers part-time and only a small portion of those will make the transition to full-time stockbrokers. Yet, in southern

California, one of our most successful regional securities firms was founded and has been managed by a former aerospace engineer and he has done quite well. So that is proof positive that engineers can make the transition to the stockbrokerage business successfully.

Engineers across the United States will be seeking new careers as our nation shifts its direction. Many engineers will prepare themselves for whatever may occur in the shrinking defense industry by joining the growing stockbrokerage industry.

POLICE AND FIRE PERSONNEL

Police and fire people are an area of part-time stockbrokers that has yet to be developed. People in these types of careers can start building an investing clientele among their co-workers, first to supplement their monthly income and then to transition to full-time stockbrokerage business as they age and desire the option of a more sedate type of work.

I have worked with several policemen and firemen first to become part-time and then full-time stockbrokers. I have always been impressed by their discipline and integrity. I have also seen these people succeed both as part-time stockbrokers and then as full-time stockbrokers because of those qualities.

Both of these professions will become examples more and more of what part-time stockbrokers will be as we move into the 21st Century of the financial services world.

REAL ESTATE AND MORTGAGE BROKERS

Real estate and mortgage brokers are hard working people dealing in a cyclical business. The real estate and mortgage businesses are noted for only two conditions: very, very good or very, very bad! Real estate and mortgage brokers work very hard to develop a customer, but once the real estate transaction is completed, the brokers do not see that customer again for a minimum of 7 years, if ever.

The real estate broker ceases following-up with his former clients because there is no more business for them. The average person does not buy a new home every year. By becoming a stockbroker part-time, real estate brokers and mortgage brokers can serve a select group of customers, customers they would have lost in the real estate business alone. Additionally, as part-time stockbrokers, they can earn some extra income to help them during the lean periods. Being a part-time stockbroker also helps the real estate and mortgage brokers maintain a relationship with the customers for the future.

With the major economic downturns taking place in the real estate business today, I see that many real estate and mortgage brokers will become part-time stockbrokers. Many will be extending their present businesses, offering to serve all of an investor's needs and not just the home or investment properties needs of their customers.

INSURANCE AGENTS

Many insurance agents have already become registered to deal in securities, mostly as financial planners or as agents for mutual funds. In the future, more and more insurance agents will become dually licensed so they can deal in securities, as well as insurance. It is not uncommon in stockbrokerage firms to have stockbrokers who also have their insurance licenses. Therefore, where I see the future development for many insurance agents is their understanding that a securities license will only enhance their ability to be a fully licensed financial consultant for their clients.

Basically, investors are becoming more and more sophisticated. A single product answer to all questions is no longer acceptable to most potential customers. Insurance agents will soon find that investors prefer to seek out only one advisor who has all types of investment products available to service their needs. Insurance agents will become stockbrokers part-time to support their present business and to expand upon their marketplace offerings.

SUMMATION

This chapter has been a brief set of examples of areas that I believe will develop the part-time stockbrokers concept into the 21st Century. Every reader of this book will also think of further extensions of the concept of personalized investment relationships. What this will mean to the Financial Services Business is substantial. As stockbrokerage firms learn to utilize the Communications Revolution that surrounds us, the concepts of decentralization will carry this concept of personalized investing out even further. I can only guess at the total affects of the future flexibility of stockbrokers on the Financial Services Industry Revolution.

My best guess is this tremendous flexibility will allow for personal relationships to be driven down to the most personal level possible, to the point where stockbrokers can be part-time and still be competitive and the mystic secrets of finance will be lifted from the world of investments. The dawning of the new age of investing is upon us.

9

THE WORLD DYNAMICS
OF THE CAPITALIST VICTORY

Earlier in this book, I talked about the failure of the economic systems of Communism and its relatives. I covered some of the affects that these failures would have upon Free Market Economics. I indicated that one of the major growth reasons for the stockbrokerage business into the 21st Century was the opportunities being presented by the reblossoming of Capitalism. This chapter will expand upon that topic and extrapolate the concepts of that opportunity of the stockbrokerage business into the 21st Century. Now, with the failure of Communism and its close relatives, Socialism and Elitism, the future of Capitalism and the stockbrokerage business is going to be dynamic.

The reader of this book has endured my ideas throughout this book. Now you are close to the end of the book and I am going to go off on what may seem like a strange tangent. The point I am trying to make is that the world's economy is going to grow beyond anyone's comprehension over the next 30 years and how, when, and where you can participate and profit.

First, a brief history background. All three of the economic concepts of Communism, Socialism, and Elitism were, in my opinion, just extensions of the economic concept of Royalism. Royalism supposedly failed at the end of World War I. It is important that I explain this perception as it will enable you to appreciate the future of Capitalism and the concepts of Free Market Economics that will economically change the world forever. It is also important because it will explain the future of the greatest economic growth in the history of mankind and the end of starvation, war, and primitive human suffering.

In the very beginning of mankind's attempts at civilization, human nature being what it is, men started enslaving each other. Back in the days of cave men, slavery was just the strong enslaving the weak to do their work. The strong then had slaves in the fields to gather and watch the crops, a task that was very simple and required little or no initiative. Hunting was still conducted by the strong because slaves were not successful at hunting.

This social structure continued as classes of rulers developed and those who were their subjects developed. The rulers tied people to the land so that they could not escape their rule. Examples would be serfdom in England and Russia.

In time, the Agricultural Revolution occurred, thus freeing up the ruling class for more leisure, education, and creativity. The additional education and creativity led to the Industrial Revolution and the creation of more goods. The initial task of the workers in the Industrial Revolution was very simple and very repetitive, watch the machine and respond to it in this way or that way.

Slavery was first tried for this type of work in the Industrial Revolution. It was discovered that slaves were not as productive as paid industrial workers. Slaves did not care and were not responsive enough to handle the simple task of industrialization. In the Southern United States, slavery was used in the fields to pick cotton, but slaves were not used at higher levels in the operations of the mills. Industrial work required more caring, dedication, and initiative.

Europe had slavery early in its history when the royalty enslaved its own people. As the Industrial Revolution expanded, a new class of people developed to handle the factories and the trade. These people came originally from the burgers (city officials) of German trading towns. These burgers organized the Trade Guilds which governed production within their cities. This new commercial class developed between the royalty (who did not work, but just ruled as was their birthright) and the slaves.

As the burgers attempted to increase productivity, they recruited talented and capable people from slavery. They created the workers unions (which were originally Trade Workers Guilds). As commerce expanded, the burgers became wealthier and more powerful. Their name evolved into the French word "bourgeoisie."

The history of Europe in the 1700 and 1800's is mostly a struggle between the powers of the royalty and the bourgeoisie. This struggle for power was hidden by many political speeches, but the reality is, people vote with their wallets.

England became a very commercial nation as its bourgeoisie became the dominant power in England. The royalty remained strong in Continental Europe as the Wars of the 1800's led up to the Great War commonly known as World War I. During the Great War, the democracies defeated the last of the great royal powers. The defeat of the Royalists supposedly ended royalty rule in 1918.

During all this violent conflict, two things occurred of great importance to the future of the 21st Century world.

ONE: THE FRENCH INTELLECTUAL DEBATES AS TO THE RIGHTS OF MAN

France was the center of all the intellectual debates concerning the rights of man. The debates centered between man's innate human rights versus the rule of the royalty to govern. This conflict can also be summarized as the Democratic Rights of the Citizens.

The debates could be crudely summarized in plain words as, "I understand that your ancestors conquered mine and have enslaved us for the last 500 years, but that was before I had a gun. Doesn't my gun make us more equal now? Now that I have a gun and can shoot you, shouldn't my opinion count in the selection of our leaders?"

These debates were being conducted in coffee shops throughout France. What were the rights of man? When the greatest peasant revolt of all times took place under the leadership of Napoleon Bonaparte (remember, Napoleon attacked the royalty of France and all the rest of Continental Europe), Napoleon replaced the royalty in most of the European nations with his new "Peasant Royalty." While this great struggle between the royal powers and the new democratic forces was going on in Europe (both the debates and the wars of democracy), a second occurrence was going on that would change the course of mankind forever.

TWO: THE DISCOVERY OF AMERICA

A new world was discovered called the Americas. It was so vast that there was land for the taking. It was so massive that you could escape into its wilderness and never be found. Freedom from the rulers was now possible. If you were bold and brave enough to go into the wilderness, you could escape slavery. This opportunity for freedom from rulers started the world's greatest migration. So great is this migration for freedom that it continues to this very day.

The first wave of the migration started in the 1600's. People being persecuted in Europe escaped to the new world from royalty rule. Then, in the 1700's, the second migration phase occurred with more people migrating to the new world escaping from debts (commercial slavery) or wars between the classes. If you were a peasant serf in Germany during the Seven Years War and the royals were going to steal all you owned and possibly kill you in a war, you might as well escape to the new world and have at least a chance at survival.

This migration to escape slavery (including commercial) expanded dramatically as stories of free land and success and opportunity drew the peasants of Europe. Peasants weary of European wars between the royalty and bourgeoisie wanted to escape.

The leaders that evolved in this new land were all students of the French Debates of Democracy. To these new leaders who had escaped slavery, the concepts of the rights of man were a given. These leaders knew their rights had been given to them by God. To the minds of these founding fathers of the new world, the rights of man were absolute. In fact, the laws of the United States today reflect the democratic debates of the rights of man.

This freedom led to a blossoming of commerce and a release of the creative genius of millions of people. People who before had been peasants, now had the freedom to prosper, the freedom to succeed or fail. Necessity being the mother of invention, these poor peasants arriving in American had only had two things: (1) necessities; and (2) their own Personal Creative Genius.

The greatest blossoming of the wealth of a society in the history of mankind took place in North America from the 1700's until this very day. Why? Not because of the political democratization of elections, but because of the democratization of <u>commerce</u>!

If we look at the United States as a nation, we have many problems today, but less than the rest of the world. Why? Because our commerce is democratized. As a nation, we have freed the Personal Creative Genius of our citizens like no other nation ever before. The freedom to create and the right to keep the fruits of your labor have created a blossoming of wealth unparalleled in the history of mankind.

We don't have slavery in the United States. This is not because we are wonderful people, we do not have slavery because it is not productive in the era of Personal Creative Genius.

The era of Personal Creative Genius is upon us now. Today, wealth is not created by slaves working in the fields. Wealth is not created by children working in textile factories. Wealth in the United States is created by individuals utilizing their Personal Creative Genius. For example, computers are worthless without software. No slave could be forced to develop software. Only a free person with the desire and passion to release their own internal personal genius to create could develop software.

The Soviets had, in reality, effective slavery. Yet, their people could not even produce enough food to feed themselves. The Soviets had no chance to compete in computers and technological commerce against people free to improvise, invent, and initiate. As the United States has freed up more and more of its citizens, it continually relearns that the more freedom people have, the more they create and the more wealth a society has.

Women did not get the political vote in the United States because men wanted to surrender control. Women got the political vote because their Personal Creative Genius was respected. Women had achieved democratic powers in commerce first, then political rights followed. Women also created wealth for society. In settling the West, building houses, and raising families, women proved their value to the creation of wealth in a commercial society. When women demanded their rights politically, most everyone knew that they had earned the rights to help govern the society that they had helped to create!

The United States, a nation of immigrants? Maybe that's one way to look at it. I prefer to look at the United States as a nation founded by dreamers. Dreamers who created wealth by doing! The founding of the United States was the second occurrence which changed the world forever. The French debates started as seeking out and defining the political rights of man. The United States then established the commercial rights of man. These events allowed commerce to become democratized. It is this irresistible trend to democratize commerce that is the greatest economic occurrence in the world today! For the next 30 years, the democratization of commerce is going to spread throughout the world and we will witness the greatest era of human advancement ever. And this area is where the greatest fortunes of the 21st Century will be made now that the struggle against royalty has finally ended.

Back to the battle for economic dominance between royalty and the bourgeoisie in Europe. World War I caused the fall of the last great royalties and the birth of political democracies in Europe. Germany, Italy, Austria, and other royals yielded to political democracy. Communism was born out of the promise of commercial freedom and political democratization. Quickly, Communism became the new tool for power of those who thought as royalty. One royalty had fallen and another royalty arose to take its place, one center of absolute power replaced another.

The political power elite everywhere in the world were in a panic after World War I. They could see that Political Democracy leads to Commercial Democracy. Commercial Democracy meant competition and a loss of their personal wealth. Commercial Democracy also leads to more Political Democracy and more Political Democracy leads to more Commercial Democracy. The power elite everywhere feared they would lose their place of importance in democratized nations. These new royals were desperate to find a system that would preserve their importance and their wealth, a Government and economic system that allowed them to keep both political and commercial power. That system was Communism or its close relative, Socialism.

Yes, if the royals promised that everything belonged to the people and that Government would take care of all of the people's needs, then the people would continue to let the power elite rule. The secret of Communism's initial success can be summarized as, "Lie to the people and tell them the end justifies the means." Every scoundrel in history has justified their criminal actions under the basis that the "end justifies the means."

Communism and Socialism are based upon the lie that the end (a better life for all) justifies the means of getting there. The means of getting there was to take away the Personal Creative Genius of the people. Every ruler in Africa, Latin America, Asia, and most of Europe saw that they could stay in power by the lie. The rulers could lie about satisfying the people's hunger for a better life by promising political democracy and then establish a system keeping all of the commercial powers through Communism or Socialism. For the good of their people, the rulers would control all national resources: land, labor, banks, telecommunications, production, travel, and permission to engage in commerce. Sounds like royalty to me.

These Royalists realized that nothing could be more dangerous than people being free to utilize their Personal Creative Genius outside the control of the rulers. This situation created the systems and conditions known as Nationalism, Communism, Socialism, and Elitism. All of these systems camouflaged an attempt by the power elite to return as ruling Royalists under the disguise of some social plan to do good for the masses. This counterattack to the concepts of the rights of man and the squelching of both commercial and political democracy peaked in 1980. In the three decades that preceded 1980, Commercial Democracy was driven out of most of Europe, Africa, Latin America, Asia, and Mexico.

The dark clouds of a return to economic and commercial rule by the ruling elite, by and through the concept of the people's Government, was overshadowing the freedom concepts of the rights of man. The basic freedom concept of the rights of man was that Personal Creative Genius creates a better world for everyone in the long run. In 1980, the United States, Canada, Hong Kong, and a few other places became the last bastions of democratic and commercial freedom on the face of the earth. At that time, elsewhere in the world, tax rates in England approached 98% of earnings for some people; those tax rates would be called confiscation of individual Personal Creative Genius. China confiscated all property of its people, declaring it was for the people's good. African and Latin American nations' Governments started to throw out the foreign devils. Those ruling elites confiscated the property of foreigners, business people, and others for the people.

The ruling Royalists all over the world were counterattacking the commercial freedoms of man under the flag of social justice. The Royalists had lost their kingdoms to the concept of political democracy. Now they were creating new kingdoms under the flags of Socialism or Communism. The rulers told the people, "We know what is best for you, so we will control all commerce. We will control housing, employment, money, travel, commerce, and you can vote for us." This was not the concept of the rights of man and political and commercial freedom!

All of this theft of property and commercial power was happening everywhere in the world in the 1950's, 60's, 70's, and 80's. However, the tide of human events was saved by two basic factors that resulted from human Personal Creative Genius.

I do love human Personal Creative Genius.

EVENT ONE: THE AMERICAN MIGRATION MIRACLE

The most creative people in each of these countries told their ruling Governments, "If you don't want me to keep what I create, then I will go to the United States where I can keep what I create." The greatest voluntary migration in the history of mankind took place between 1960 and today. The English called this massive migration of England's best and brightest people out of England into the United States the "Brain Drain." Europe, Africa, Asia, and Latin America also saw their best people start to migrate to the United States. Engineers, doctors, scientists, technicians, business people, dreamers, wanters, and doers all headed for the promised land known as the United States. There they could keep the rewards of their own Personal Creative Genius.

In Africa, the nation of Ghana was once one of the wealthiest nations in the world (1600- 1700's). Ghana was so rich that it was called the Gold Coast. Europeans fought and died to trade with Ghana. The nation of Ghana under British Administration was a very wealthy part of Africa. Using their independence as justification, Ghana transformed itself into a Communist/Socialist state. The nation of Ghana had created thousands of medical doctors, but you cannot find many doctors in Ghana today. Why? They are in New York where they can work and earn bigger paychecks. These doctors can now earn more after taxes and have greater freedom to develop their Personal Creative Genius in a Commercial Democracy. Their efforts in the United States and Personal Creative Genius can develop greater wealth for them and their family. Also, the United States is enriched by having the services of these intelligent, highly talented doctors.

In the last 30 years, as nation after nation has became an Elitist ruling state under the claims of Communism, Socialism, or Nationalism (where Government controls commerce for the good of the people of just that nation), the people of those nations have become poorer. The nations themselves have also become poorer because the people with Personal Creative Genius have been the first to escape to the United States.

If the United States had developed a plan to attempt to steal the most brilliant people away from these nations, every nation on Earth would have fought a war with the United States. Every nation would have fought to keep the United States from stealing their irreplaceable natural resources, their human geniuses, from being taken away from their society. Yet, the ruling Elitists of those countries wanted these people gone.

The ruling Elitists wanted the geniuses gone because they knew that these brilliant people believed that Commercial Democracy was a human right and, thus, these brilliant people were a danger to the Elitist rule. So these nations voluntarily sent the United States many of their best and the brightest people. From Europe, Asia, Africa, and Latin America, millions of intelligent people fled to the United States. What a wonderful gift these underdeveloped nations gave to the United States! The United States should have changed the phrase on the Statue of Liberty from, "Send me your poor and downtrodden," to, "Send me your best and brightest." Millions of immigrants came to America with intelligence, the passion to succeed, and love and respect for Commercial Democracy. The United States has blossomed from this migration beyond any economic measure of mere numbers. This great migration is one of the reasons that the United States is now positioned for its greatest economic expansion ever!

Yet, it was the second result of human Personal Creative Genius that is causing the collapse of the Royalist Elite concept of Governments everywhere in the world today and causing the beginning of the greatest economic expansion ever.

EVENT TWO: THE COMMUNICATIONS REVOLUTION

Agriculture could easily be ruled by landlords, armies, and the use of force. A landed peasant could be watched and his food stocks could be taken away by force at the orders of the rulers. The Industrial Revolution was much more difficult to rule. This was because factories could be moved and goods could be transported away from the threats of confiscation by Government. Yet, the most difficult area to rule was creative people. The reason was that the most productive people in an industrial society were those people had the freedom to create new products and concepts and were the most mobile.

Now in the 1970's and 80's, along comes the Communications Revolution, supported by the Computer Revolution. No longer could Governments keep secrets or lies from the people, the truth was becoming obvious to all. The nations and their people have been suffering under Elitist rulers. The Elitist lie of the public's eventual prosperity under the rule of the Elitist was proven to be false. The promised end was vanishing and the subjects of the Elitist rule saw the reality of the cruelty that had been placed upon them. These people had been made slaves again, under the promise of social justice.

All of a sudden, everyone could plainly see the truth: That people who are allowed to be free to prosper, succeed! People who are able to resolve their own necessities and utilize their Personal Creative Genius can become wealthy. The truth that free people can become rich is now self-evident. The fact that Commercial Democracy is a right of man is now a concept whose time has come.

I recently read that the United States Government's Central Intelligence Agency (the CIA) accredited the fall of Communism to the VCR. The CIA knew that, as VCRs saturated the former Soviet Union, common people throughout the nation could see with their own eyes the truth that other people had cars, stores had food, and countries had hospitals that cured people instead of killing them. Most important, American movies taught the people of the former Soviet Union about the American attitude of "Do It Yourself." The do it yourself attitude generated results. The do it yourself attitude is an excellent example of Commercial Democracy and Personal Creative Genius.

The Communications Revolution also informed the rest of the world that you are better off taking care of yourself than waiting for your rulers to give you something. While the Communications Revolution has been building up steam towards Commercial Democracy, the rulers of the nations under the flag of social justice enriched themselves beyond comprehension. These rulers gave great speeches of their caring for the people and their nation while they controlled the commerce and stole the wealth.

The wealth of the Communist Leaders, African Dictators, and Latin American Generals at the expense of their people can be demonstrated by the example of President Marcos in the Philippines. Marcos was not a rich man when he entered politics in the Philippines. He was a devout anti-Communist, yet he propagated programs and policies of Royal Elitist Economics in the Philippines. Marcos wanted to restrict competition through: (1) Nationalism (restrict foreign competition); (2) heavy regulation of commerce; (3) the permitting processes for commerce; and (4) regulator harassment of internal competitors.

Marcos stopped the democratization of commerce in the Philippines in 1972 by making most commercial and Governmental decisions. Marcos became one of the wealthiest men on Earth. While Marcos counted his money, the Filipino people slipped from the second wealthiest nation in Asia (earning in 1941, 80% of what the average Japanese person earned) to the poorest non-Communist nation in Asia (earning 1/80th of what the average Japanese person earned in 1990).

During Marcos' rule, the Philippines exported to America almost 3,000,000 people. Some of the Philippines' brightest and most capable people fled to the United States: accountants, lawyers, doctors, engineers, nurses, business people, and others. Besides those who escaped to the United States, another 3,000,000 escaped to Europe, the Middle East, and other parts of Asia. Almost 10% of the population of the Philippines has been forced to pursue the development of their own Personal Creative Genius outside of their homeland.

The citizens of the Philippines were forced to flee not because of Communism or Socialism, but because of the same ruling royalty mindset of Elitism. Elitism justifies the proposition that the power elite rule over the citizens of a nation. The basis of the Elitist rulers' authority was under the guise of their concern for social justice. The Elitist definition of social justice was their desire to do good for the people of their nation, not freedom for those people to do what they believed was best for themselves. History has shown everyone that the only people who do well under the rule of Elitists, are the Elitists themselves.

The Communications Revolution has occurred as the result of Personal Creative Genius. The Communications Revolution is a great invention of equipment, systems, lifestyle, and passion of the common person for knowledge. This event has brought the truth to the eyes and minds of millions around the world that the greatest poverty in the world is not a lack of material things, but a lack of hope.

Despair is the only thing that the Communist, Socialist, and Nationalist rules created for their people. The Communications Revolution is returning to these people hope, vision, and opportunity to participate in a better life through the utilization of their own Personal Creative Genius.

Commercial Democracy is being developed and fostered under the Communications Revolution. Rulers can no longer keep the truth from their people. People everywhere are learning that help to develop a better life for most people in the world is only a phone call away. Satellites can transmit data to the center of Africa to show farmers how to stop the disease that is destroying their lives. A mother in Central Asia can watch a satellite transmission on prenatal care translated into her native language to educate her on how to take care of herself and her baby.

The dawning of the greatest economic expansion in the history of the world is founded upon the Communications Revolution. The Communications Revolution is fostering the expansion of Commercial Democracy throughout the world. The entire world is now awakening to the French Revolution's concept of the rights of man. Not just the political right to vote, but the right to prosper and be happy, the commercial rights to utilize their own Personal Creative Genius to make a better life for themselves and their families. Billions of people are now free to make a better life for themselves today. And this means the rest of the world will be a better place in the process.

In the brilliant books written by the French economist, Fernand Braudel, <u>Civilization & Capitalism</u>, on the economic history of the world of commerce from the 1400's through the 1700's, Mr. Braudel stated that when the English arrived in India in the 1600's, the average person in India was wealthier than the average person in Britain. The very reason that the British were in India was to obtain some of the wealth of India and take it home to Britain. Similarly, the wealth of China drew the Europeans to seek its riches. Today, people talk about the poverty of China and India as if these lands and people have failed. People seem to think that China and India have failed to create wealth and are now doomed to a life of poverty forever. WRONG!

I predict tremendous economic growth in the world's economies that will, within 30 years (2022), increase the average personal wealth (personal GNP) in the world overall to be within 70% of that of the United States at that time. Today, I would guess that the personal GNP average in the world is about 15% of that of the United States.

Now for the really exciting news for all of you Doubting Thomases. I also predict that the United States will enter into its greatest economic expansion ever during the next 30 years. During the late 1990's and early 2000's, the United States' economy will be growing at the real rate of 10% per year. Yes, you heard it here first folks, the beginning of the greatest economic growth phase in the history of mankind, the democratization of commerce throughout the world. Everyone can participate: African, Asian, educated, uneducated, young, old, male, or female.

The United States' economy still has several years of economic adjustments to make from a war-time economy to a peace-time economy. At the same time, the Communications Revolution is opening up new markets for development of Commercial Democracy throughout the world. People want to live better and now they know they can if they take action in their own hands and utilize their own Personal Creative Genius to create a better world.

Look at the world today: The United States, Western Europe, Japan, and a few other places are entering the 21st Century. Food is a given in these places as are basic medical care, shelter, and education for all. We in the developed world struggle with wealth and its new diseases of drugs, crime, and change, while most of the rest of the world struggles with the problems of 1918, or 1940, or 1960. These people are struggling with the same problems that existed when their nations started to follow Elitist policies. These nations are still trapped in the 20th Century.

For example, Eastern Europe is in a commercial time warp of 1940. Similarly, the Russians and their colonies are trapped in a commercial time warp of 1918 with its problems of starvation and lack of shelter. Latin America's nations became trapped in a commercial time warp of the 1950's to the 1960's when they abandoned the American dream of personal freedom for the lies of Socialism. Africa is also trapped in the 1950's as its rulers are still determined to build steel plants that were a sign of power in 1950, but today are relics of yesterday.

What all of this means concerning the great economic growth for the next 30 years and why the United States will prosper so greatly is that the underdeveloped nations of the world can develop very quickly. In short, the underdeveloped world can cover a great amount of development very quickly utilizing the Communications Revolution. These underdeveloped nations can accomplish in 30 years what before would have taken them 100 years.

The newly freed economy of Russia can grow at 30% per year as its freed people utilize their own Personal Creative Genius and create wealth. These freed people can learn from the Communications Revolution the secrets of expeditious development and, in 30 years, Russia can become a wealthy nation again, as it always should have been.

China today is really two different commercial nations. One part of China has economic freedom. That part is growing at 18 to 30% per year and its people are becoming wealthier. However, the other part of China is still Communist and very poor as people are not allowed to prosper. Through the Communications Revolution, these people can all participate in the democratization of commerce as soon as they are free.

Yes, I believe that all the people of these great nations are going to prosper. Their economic growth will be very rapid as they quickly catch up to the rest of the world. I believe this growth will come easier and faster than historically because the financially unfortunate nations have the advantage of simply copying the western nations, such as the United States, Western Europe, Japan, and Hong Kong.

Imagine the 4.5 billion people of the underdeveloped world getting wealthier at the rate of 18 to 30% per year! What a wonderful opportunity! Especially for the United States. The United States will prosper the most as it becomes the primary supplier to these developing nations and their people for the following reasons:

1.   The United States is the world's cultural and commercial leader.

People everywhere in the world will want to be like the United States because we are the world's cultural leader. The world's people will purchase their cultural commerce from the United States. One of the major reasons that the United States is so dominant, culturally and commercially, in the world today is that we have the most flexible culture in the history of mankind. Anything that works or is good, we, in the United States, accept without hesitation as our own. Examples of some areas where American culture dominates are: pizza, Mexican food, sushi, music like the Beatles and La Bamba, skateboards, surfboards, and more.

The United States may be seen as a large test marketplace in the world for what sells well. There are more Chinese restaurant chains in the United States than in China. There are more Thai Restaurant chains in the States than in Thailand. The United States is the world's cultural leader because we shamelessly accept what works and claim it as our own. The rest of the world can come shopping here and see it all, choose what they like, and take it home, with instructions on how to assemble and operate. The United States will be the number one supplier to the development of the world over the next 30 years because we have what they want!

2.   The Democratization of technology.

In many places in the world, certain people have maintained their importance or power and influence by controlling technology. The more sophisticated and difficult the operation of something, the more important these people have made themselves seem. For example, "Only Engineer Gonzales can handle that piece of equipment because it is so complicated." This made Engineer Gonzales appear important, almost omnipotent. Well, in the United States, our personal computer manufacturers discovered people do not purchase what they cannot understand or use. So the United States' personal computer industry developed the term "User Friendly." This means that the computer is friendly to the average user and you do not have to be a computer genius to use a personal computer.

Well, for some of us in the United States (such as myself), computers were still too difficult to understand. Then Apple Computer created a personal computer system so user friendly that I refer to it as "my stupid buddy system." Apple recognized that the paying customers may not understand computer language and designed a computer to help us (the users) accomplish computing tasks very easily. Example: The computer says, "Roll the mouse until the arrow on the screen is in the box that says off." Not complicated, even I understand this. I give a great deal of credit to Apple Computer for establishing the democratization of technology and for bringing down the level of technological wonder to the level of the average person. Apple Computer started the race to make technology understandable to everyone. This is an example of the democratization of technology.

As the people in the rest of the world decide to purchase capital equipment, systems, goods, and services, I believe that beyond a shadow of doubt, they will seek out only that which they can understand. In this category, the United States' suppliers are unmatched. Only the Asian computer companies have grasped this concept and are starting to close the gap and this is only because they sell so much of their product to the States. The average person doesn't want to have to learn FORTRAN to make an axle for a truck. They want a production system that will say, "Hi. What size axles do you want today?" and then do all the rest. The world will do their shopping for their development in the United States because we have the easiest goods to work with.

3.   The United States has some of the developing nations' best citizens located in the United States to conduct commerce between the nations.

Already, the United States has millions of citizens from those developing countries here to show us how to do business back there, in their original homeland. Three million Filipinos, two million Indians, hundreds of thousands of Poles, Russians, Ukrainians, Turks, Iranians, Africans, Vietnamese, Pakistani, Chinese, Guyanese, and more.

Guyana in South America is a perfect example. A nation of great potential wealth for its citizens, Guyana pursued Socialism and forced out some 300,000 of its best citizens who came to live in the United States. That's almost 30% of the total population of Guyana! When the Government of Guyana starts to open up to Commercial Democracy, its commercial development will be led by the Guyanese-Americans. These Guyanese-American people will return to Guyana with ideas, capital, contacts, energy, and experience. What would have taken Guyana 100 years to achieve, will take these Guyanese-Americans less than 30 years.

Once these Guyanese-Americans start to rebuild their homeland, you are looking at economic growth of 30% per year or better for Guyana. You can envision renewed wealth for the people of Guyana and the American suppliers that support that growth.

It is so true that the United States has benefitted from the massive inflow of immigrant population over the last 30 years. Now, again, the United States will benefit as these people help rebuild their original homeland from the suppliers in the United States whom they know and do business with.

In the year 2022 (30 years from now), I know that I will see residential community developments in the Philippines, Africa, and Latin America that will rival anything in southern California for their quality of lifestyle and beauty. These residential community developments will be the results of copying what is best in the United States and replanting it back in those countries.

You will recall that, earlier in this book, I stated that I believe the biggest business in the world is going to be the international retirement business. If an American worker can retire in the sunshine of Mexico, Africa, the Philippines, or India at 1/5 the cost of retiring in California and still enjoy all of the same lifestyle benefits, you are going to see the greatest reverse migration in the history of the world. I predict that 30 million people from the OECD nations (the industrial nations) will retire into resort communities in the undeveloped world by the year 2025. That will make the international retirement business the biggest business in the world and the most profitable. The world is a small place and getting smaller every day as technology continues to grow, the cross border flow of people and commerce is just getting started and the primary benefactor will be the United States.

4.   The United States will be the primary supplier of financial capital.

The United States will be the primary benefactor of all this worldwide growth because the United States is going to be the primary supplier of financial capital for these new Capitalist economies. We are going to supply the equipment and the money to develop the world into the 21st Century. The United States will be in the 21st Century what England was in the 19th Century: the commercial and financial center of the world. As the rest of the world's nations start to open their economies, they will need the capital market expertise of those in the United States to finance their development.

If you put all of these factors together you reach the same conclusion that I do. The world's Capitalist Revolution will be great for the United States and the world. It will be especially good for United States stockbrokers.

THE UNITED STATES STOCKBROKERS ROLE IN THESE DEVELOPMENTS.

There are hundreds of examples to support my conclusion here. The best example is the Philippines. The Philippines will serve as my primary example to demonstrate what I foresee in the future for the 21st Century Stockbroker. The Philippines' opportunities are the greatest because of all the cross border opportunities for stockbrokers.

Over three million Filipinos live within the United States today. These Filipino-Americans have created about 700,000 households. The heads of these households are often doctors, lawyers, accountants, engineers, nurses, and other highly paid professionals. I will estimate that the average household income of a Filipino-American is approximately $47,000 per year, higher than the average U.S. citizen. Interesting to note is that Filipino-Americans have a very high savings rate, similar to most immigrant groups in the United States. I have read that the Filipino-American's average savings rate is approximately 27% of their after-tax earnings which I estimate at $30,000 per year. So if Filipino-Americans are savings 27% of $30,000 per year, that equals personal savings of $8,100 per year. With 700,000 households, that means the gross savings of all Filipino-Americans could approach 5.6 billion dollars per year.

The present interest rates on bank savings accounts in the United States is around 3% per year. The average return on equity of a company on the Philippine Stock Exchange is over 33% per year. The businesses in the Philippines desperately need financial capital to finance their growth and development.

Illustration: Philippine companies want to purchase capital equipment from the United States to generate electrical power for the Philippines. Investment returns of 33% per year or higher are common because of the shortage of financial capital in the Philippines. It seems obvious that the company that creates the financial services ability to offer the Filipinos in America a 33% return on their investments and savings will do quite well. Instead of earning only 3% annually on their money, these Filipino-Americans will earn much higher investment returns. Besides the Filipino-Americans making a lot of money on their investments, they will be helping out both the Philippines and the United States in their commercial development. The stockbrokerage firm that captures this one area of business could profit quite nicely over the next 30 years.

Recognize that I am not saying that the Filipino-Americans will invest all of their guesstimate 5.6 billion dollars of annual savings into Philippines opportunities. If, for example, the Filipino-Americans place 80% of their savings in safer savings ventures within the United States and place only 20% in the Philippines, the sum is still over <u>one billion dollars</u> per year of new investments into the Philippines. Obviously, still a very big number for any developing country.

At Montano Securities Corporation, one of our major projects is to recruit and develop stockbrokers for our firm who can service this unique and outstanding opportunity. We see where this opportunity exists for the Philippines, Taiwan, China, Korea, Indonesia, Vietnam, Thailand, Malaysia, India, Pakistan, Iran, Turkey, Ukraine, Russia, Romania, Bulgaria, all of the African nations, Latin America, and others. We have made it one of our top business priorities to create an ethnic securities distribution system within the United States. We believe that this commercial situation will be crucial for the development of many nations.

There are many areas of difficulty in developing these cross border capital markets. Some difficulties are the laws and accounting and banking systems in many underdeveloped countries. This is why I have lectured in 48 countries on this subject over the last 25 years. My associates and I have even given seminars on how to develop capital markets in some nations with statues of Lenin standing behind us and secret police following us everywhere we went.

We have seen the situation and business opportunities from Guyana, to Bolivia, to Moscow, to India, to Mindanao, Philippines. We understand the tremendous business opportunity that exists to be developed. The world is starting its greatest economic growth phase ever and it needs Capitalists to do that. The greatest Capitalists in the world are from the United States and that is the future of the 21st Century Stockbroker!

CONCLUSION

I want to reiterate some very important points in conclusion of this subject of the dynamics of the world's Capitalist Revolution. First, I want to clarify that the revolution is just getting started. Second, this will be one of the biggest, most exciting, profitable, and rewarding areas of commerce ever. As five billion people around the world now become free to utilize their Personal Creative Genius, they will accelerate the economic growth of the rest of the world in ways previously unparalleled. Third, the United States will become the primary benefactor of this world economic boom as it supplies that commercial democratization of the world with equipment, services, and financial capital. Fourth, the United States stockbrokerage business will be the major catalyst of this commercial dynamism as it brings together all of the components of development and then sparks them with investment capital.

I have no doubt that 30 years from now, in the year 2023, when I am 75 years old (assuming of course that I am still here), someone will say how lucky I was to have made all the profits and money on these business programs. That person will say how lucky I was to have developed this international capital markets system. That same person may also say that I made that money upon the backs of the poor and downtrodden of the world. I may even be accused of having made a profit off the poor Filipinos.

Yet I will always know, as you will know, that few see what I have described here and even fewer believe. In 30 years, when a child in the Philippines turns on his light switch, he will not say, "Thank you, Dan Montano and other Filipino-American investors for giving me lights to read by." This child will only hear his parents complain about the cost of electrical power.

When a woman goes to the supermarket in Africa and can choose between many types of fish to purchase, she will still complain about the price of fish. She will not thank me or the investors who financed the building of the supermarket, the trucks that delivered the fish, the ships that caught the fish, and the cannery that prepared the fish.

These situations are O.K., even welcome, because we will know that we have made the world a better place and that we have profited from our utilization of our own Personal Creative Genius. We envisioned the trends that created the democratization of commerce and Capitalism and the greatest economic expansion ever. We will deserve our profits and we will have helped to create a better world. It is a great time to be a stockbroker because the next 30 years will be a period of economic rewards and excitement and because the whole world needs us!

10

THE OVERVIEW OF THE NEXT 30 YEARS FOR THE STOCKBROKERAGE BUSINESS

This book is about the 21st Century Stockbroker - a New Wave, the Catalyst of the World's Economic and Financial Revolution. We have previously discussed the direction of current major economic and cultural trends into and through our present day commercial culture. Now, I will extend the culmination of those trends into the future.

The first chapters of this book started with a description of the Financial Services Industry and the changes occurring there. Then we moved on to the revolutionary changes developing within the Financial Services Business. Next, we reviewed the stockbrokerage business of today and tomorrow, looking at the new marketplace potentials. This led to analysis of the niche marketplace opportunities within the United States securities business. We then discussed how these factors will evolve into the world's greatest economic boom and, last, the stockbroker's role in facilitating the greatest economic expansion in the history of mankind.

Basically, we started this book with the concept of one brick of the securities business upon which I have built the conclusion that stockbrokers are going to save the world. At the end of the last chapter on the effects of the Victory of World Capitalism, the reader is standing upon a mountain looking down into the valley and wondering how I got them to that position.

With this chapter, the overview of the next 30 years, I want to start at the mountaintop and go back down the specific processes to the basics. When I was preparing this book, I decided that to start from the big picture and work down would make it more difficult for the reader to accept my premises. Starting with the simple and obvious trends and building up to the bigger picture would make it easier for readers to accept my train of logic.

This chapter is the summation of the next 30 years of economic and commercial growth for the world as I see it. This chapter will take the big picture and release upon the reader the overwhelming realization of the massive forces at work today that will change the world forever!

The future that I foresee for the world and its people is not a mere possibility, but a fact of the future! The last 70 years have been a nightmare from which the world is now awakening. History has proven time and time again the brilliance of humans. There is no doubt in my mind that God gave humans a Personal Creative Genius so they could solve all of the problems they encountered.

Every time in the course of history, humans have risen to greatness to resolve the difficulties that confronted them. Today, we actually have two separate worlds: A free and rich world and a economically enslaved and poor world. An estimated 1.5 million people died in the world this year from malaria. Malaria is a disease that is easily cured in the rich parts of the world. Those 1.5 million people dying every year could be the ones possessing the Personal Creative Genius to solve cancer, or develop light travel, or to explain the purpose of life.

We, the world's population, have sacrificed so much of our human wealth out of pure stupidity. Ignorance kills and destroys more than all other factors combined. Now, with the realization of the total failure of Elitist Economics, Nationalism, Socialism, Central Planning, and Communism, the world is repositioned for the great reawakening of true social justice. True social justice occurs when everyone has a chance to make their own lives and the lives of others better.

The United States is the world's only military might today. The United States is also the world's only economic might, if you include our commercial clones of Japan, Germany, France, Italy, the Netherlands, and Britain. These nations are commercial clones in the sense that we all share Commercial Democracy. What does the commercial greatness of these nations derive itself from? One thing: <u>competition</u>!

I know poverty. My brother and I were born poor. I know hunger.

I remember going to school with holes in my shoes for months. I remember placing cardboard paper in the holes and painting it black so that no one would know that I had holes in my shoes. (One small example of Personal Creative Genius.) The only thing that lifted my brother and I out of poverty was Commercial Democracy. Commercial Democracy in the United States allowed us to compete equally and from competition, we succeeded.

My brother and I worked 6 to 7 days a week. We started at 5:00 a.m. and worked until 1:00 or 2:00 a.m. Every task to earn money we undertook, we worked as cooks, field hands, laborers, salesman, truck drivers, and more. If someone wanted something done, we said yes, no matter what it was, then we figured out how to do it. We competed for everything. We delivered results and we prospered.

Were we unique? NO!

We were just common people. Just like you. Average people who just wanted more for our lives. The same basic motivation as thousands of people I have met throughout the world. Most of the people reading this book know what I mean. You understand the desires and the needs to make your life and your children's lives better and more fulfilling.

You have worked hard, studied hard, sacrificed, and invested in yourselves. You know how hard you worked to get where you are. You remember the cold, dark mornings when you woke up before the sun to start work. You remember the emptiness in your heart when you left for work while everyone else was still asleep. You know the commitment that you made to improve your life and the lives of your children. You remember the lonely price you paid in attempting to better your life.

For all the pains of that struggle, you have succeeded. Of course, there is still more for you to do with your life. Yet, by your efforts you have lifted yourself up. Yes, you are a very special person. Unique within the world. NO!

Billions of people throughout this world are just like you and me. They are willing to work, to study, to sacrifice, and to invest in their tomorrows. For the last 70 years, these people have been unable to compete and prosper. They have been unable to work, to grow, or to succeed. Now all that is changing. Billions of people will be free to utilize their God given Personal Creative Genius to better their lives and the lives of others. The amount of human energy and Personal Creative Genius that will be released over the next 30 years will be beyond comprehension.

The best example to provide of this is South China. In 1980,

South China started to open up to Free Market Economics. Once freed to be able to improve their lives, the people of South China have exceeded everyone's highest expectations. Some international economist stated that the economic growth of South China has been between 15% and 30% per year. For the last 12 years, the people of South China have generated economic wealth for themselves at the ever increasing rate of 15 to 30% per year. These people have utilized their individual Personal Creative Genius and created a better life for themselves and their families. What they have started in South China is going to continue for the next 30 years or better, not only in South China, but throughout the world.

What has happened in South China will happen everywhere in the world where people are freed to prosper. Africa is poor today, yet it has tremendous natural resources. The African people have long histories of great civilizations and great inventions. Africa should not be poor. It is only the Governments of Africa that have made it poor by denying the people freedom to prosper. As the people of Africa are freed to prosper, they will! They will utilize their individual Personal Creative Genius to create a better world for themselves and their families.

Over 80% of the world's people are poor today, the same 80% who have suffered under Elitist economical policies. Now, these people are being freed to utilize their individual Personal Creative Genius. As the nations of the world free up the natural genius of their people, their nations' economies will grow at 15 to 30% per year. This means that the entire world's cumulative economy will be lifted. As the overall world economy grows at these rates of 15 to 30 % per year, world trade will boom. The United States, the Western European nations, and Japan will prosper as they will be the primary providers of the equipment and expertise for this worldwide expansion.

As the world starts to rebuild from the days of economic slavery, another major event will occur. Millions of European, American, and Japanese retirees will migrate to the warmer underdeveloped world to retire in luxury. This mass migration of the educated and affluent will stimulate the transfer of wealth and technology from rich nations to poor nations. This will enhance the greatest economic growth ever and return the world to a more evenly developed world. Medical centers in Mexico, Ghana, the Philippines, China, and India will be as good as any in California. The same equipment and doctors, operated by the same hospital company, will be serving retirees from California to Manchester to Tokyo to Hamburg.

The only thing missing for these wonderful events to occur is financial capital. That financial capital surplus exists in the United States along with the expertise to analyze, allocate, and transfer that capital. The United States has the stockbrokerage talents, expertise, and ability to perform in this role. Over the next 30 years, the Financial Services Industry within the United States will be the catalyst to the greatest economic boom the world has ever seen.

The internal and external competitive pressures will change the United States Financial Services Business. As the Commercial Banks are attacked by competitors from all sides, the Financial Services Business will lean towards the advantages that stockbrokers possess. The stockbrokers will be handling the financing of the greatest economic growth of the world and the United States. As the primary provider of financial capital to the businesses of the United States and the world, stockbrokers will also prosper.

This quick overview which peeks into the future of the next 30 years is from the perspective of the worldwide big picture. It comes down to the simple fact that stockbrokers in the United States will be the New Wave of change and the catalyst to these dynamic economic, commercial, and financial times.

An analogy about the future economy of the world that is self-evident to me is the following: The developed world is like a mountain range covered by snow. The undeveloped world is like a desert at the foot of those mountains. The desert is lifeless and poor. As the sun melts the snow, the resulting water will flow down the mountains into the desert. If that water is channeled intelligently to irrigate the desert, the desert will blossom, bringing life and riches. Stockbrokers are the business professionals who are responsible for channeling financial capital. Free to do their job, stockbrokers of the world will make the world's economy blossom as never before.

Stockbrokers are the future catalyst of the world's Economic and Financial Revolution. The 21st Century Stockbroker is more than a business person who makes a lot of money. He or she is also the key to the success of the world's transformation from a world with 80% of its people commercially enslaved and living in poverty with needless death and suffering to the Star Trek Economy!

The potential of the Star Trek Economy is upon us. Stockbrokers will cut the path to the future economy just as they always have. You should consider becoming a stockbroker and participating in the greatest business in the world. Of course, you will enjoy great pay and prestige. But even more important, it is a business dealing in tomorrow, an exciting, dynamic business where your Personal Creative Genius can blossom and bear fruit for you and all mankind.

The 21st Century Stockbroker is you!

11

HOW TO
BECOME A
STOCKBROKER

This book has been directed at how great the stockbrokerage business is today and will continue to be tomorrow and the role stockbrokers will play in the rapidly changing world of finance into the 21st Century. This chapter is a very basic chapter which explains how a person can become a stockbroker in the United States. This chapter will only deal with the United States' system of becoming a stockbroker.

In the United States, there is one major regulatory obstacle in the process of becoming a stockbroker. The process is primarily governed by the National Association of Securities Dealers (NASD). The NASD has been entrusted as a self-regulatory agency by the United States Government to oversee the securities industry within the United States. The NASD qualifies individuals as stockbrokers by administering an examination. This examination is the only major obstacle that is required to become a registered representative (a stockbroker) in the United States.

Due to the fact that passing this examination is the main hurdle to becoming a stockbroker in the United States, a more detailed analysis of the examination is required. The NASD administers several different examinations for different levels of qualifications. Each examination covers and/or tests different areas of knowledge about the securities industry and its practices. The primary examination to become a fully registered stockbroker in the United States is referred to as the Series 7 Examination. It is considered by many to be the most difficult of the examinations given by the NASD. Essentially, the Series 7 Examination covers a full spectrum of the securities industry and its practices, making it a full qualification examination for those wishing to deal as a full service stockbroker.

The NASD Series 7 Examination consists of 250 multiple choice questions. Generally, there are 4 answer choices for each multiple choice question. A 6 hour time limit is established for taking the entire examination. The 6 hours allowed for the examination is divided into two concurrent 3 hour sessions. A half-hour to a 1 hour break between the two sessions is required. The NASD Series 7 Examination is a computer-based examination given at different computer centers around the United States. The test is administered Monday through Saturday, with the exception of holidays, during normal business hours.

To pass the Series 7 Examination, a score of 70% or higher must be obtained. The national passing rate for the examination is over 50%. However, it is very common for people to have to take the exam 2 or 3 times before they are successful in passing. The NASD Series 7 Examination, unfortunately, has a history for asking questions in a round-about or tricky manner. This is one of the reasons the examination is considered difficult.

Although the examination is passable, the most pressing concern is generally the vast amount of information and the complex subject matter that will be covered in the examination. It has been our experience in preparing for the examination that a division of the various areas of coverage into 9 distinct categories of the securities business is most logical. This organization of the material to be studied will also aid in the comprehension and understanding of the material.

The 9 categories can be divided into:

1. Corporate Securities
2. Government Securities
3. Municipal Securities
4. Regulations
    (a) Securities Act of 1933
    (b) Securities Exchange Act of 1934
    (c) NASD Rules and Regulations
    (d) Municipal Rules and Regulations

5. Securities Analysis & Economic Analysis
6. Taxes & Tax Advantaged Investments
7. Investment Accounts and Execution Procedures
8. Options
9. Mutual Funds

The NASD Series 7 Examination is the most difficult hurdle to becoming a stockbroker. But to qualify to sit and take the examination, a person must first be sponsored by a qualified and registered member NASD stockbrokerage firm. Given that the securities industry is a heavily regulated industry, all active stockbrokers must be supervised and managed to ensure that securities laws are not broken. Thus, even before taking the examination, a position must be offered to an applicant by an NASD Member stockbrokerage firm. That stockbrokerage firm must be willing to commit and take the responsibility of managing and supervising the potential stockbroker's activities. Each stockbrokerage firm has its own procedures to distinguish which applicants it will be willing to sponsor. Regardless of an applicant's desire to become a stockbroker, he or she must first utilize their efforts in obtaining sponsorship from a NASD Member firm to ensure the opportunity to take the examination.

Upon commitment of sponsorship by an NASD Member firm, an individual must register with the NASD. To register with the NASD to take the examination, an applicant must file a form known as the Form U-4. With the filing of the Form U-4 with the NASD, a personnel file will be opened at the NASD for every applicant. This NASD file will follow the applicant wherever he or she goes in the securities industry.

The filing of the U-4 Form with the NASD will cause certain parts of that documentation to be sent to the United States Government's Securities & Exchange Commission (SEC) and the Federal Bureau of Investigation (FBI). The Form U-4 will then be reviewed and processed. On average, it takes approximately 4 weeks for processing. This time allows for any additional required disclosures to be supplied and corrections to any information to be made by the regulators.

Upon the completion of this application process, the NASD provides the applicant a 3 month time period in which to sit for the NASD Series 7 Examination. Thus, during this 3 month time period, a computer terminal can be reserved by the applicant to take the NASD Series 7 Examination at one of the test centers. Should this 3 month time period expire before the examination is taken, a supplemental application must be submitted to receive an additional 3 month test window.

Unfortunately, many applicants do not pass the examination on their first attempt. Should this occur, a mandatory 30 day waiting period is required, thus freezing the applicant for 30 days before the examination can be retaken. If, after 3 attempts at the examination, the applicant has still not passed, a 6 month freeze is issued. Thus, 6 more months must pass until the test can be retaken.

If the examination is completed and a score of 70% or better is achieved, the computer terminal will notify you immediately of having passed. The NASD will receive your test results and notify your NASD Member sponsoring stockbrokerage firm of the results. On average, a further 2 weeks is required from passing the examination to becoming fully registered and licensed with the NASD as a stockbroker.

The main obstacle in passing the NASD Series 7 Examination is obtaining the required training to take the exam. Training for this examination is crucial and the most important aspect in preparing to become a stockbroker. Various courses, both correspondent and self-study, are offered by different institutes and companies around the United States. At Montano Securities Corporation, we have learned that the investment in training for the Series 7 Examination is crucial to success. Therefore, we have developed our own program at Montano Securities Corporation to train people for this examination. Our training program has been dramatically successful!

The first difficulty that we tackled is the depth of information required to pass the exam. To handle this wide and diverse scope of material, we divided the subject matter into 9 primary topics to be discussed separately. Our training program is outlined as follows:

CLASS 1: CORPORATE STOCKS AND MONEY MARKET INSTRUMENTS

This material sets a strong foundation through the coverage of common stocks, stock splits, dividends, rights and risks, as well as preferred stocks. The basic money market instruments such as commercial paper and bankers acceptances also augment the topic when discussing short term investments.

Class 2: Bonds: Corporate, Government, and Municipal

This section covers all the mechanics of bonds, including their purpose, advantages, disadvantages, and comparisons between corporate, municipal, and government. Other training programs approach this material in separate courses. We have found that a session dedicated to debt instruments, where the different types can be compared, has proven worthwhile and more beneficial to the student. Corporate bonds and municipal bonds especially have traditionally been heavily tested topics on the NASD Series 7 Examination.

Class 3: Investment Companies and Mutual Funds

This class discusses the different types of investment companies and focuses in on mutual funds and their advantages.

Class 4: Investment Banking and Securities Trading

This is one of the more interesting topics to discuss. The mechanics of being a stockbroker are explained and the excitement of investment banking is always evident. We have put emphasis on the NASDAQ market given that it is often the most difficult area to understand and it is the area we believe the future of the securities markets is evolving to.

Class 5: Analysis and the Financial Press

This material is based on basic economic, technical, and fundamental analysis. Simple accounting backgrounds are also utilized. During the course of the NASD Series 7 Examination, an exhibit book is often utilized, and, as such, this class is geared to prepare the trainee for that event.

Class 6: Rules and Regulations

This section discusses the rules and regulations that pertain to being a stockbroker. This has historically been a heavily tested area and we therefore spend a good amount of time discussing the securities acts, the self-regulatory organizations, as well as the exchange rules and procedures.

CLASS 7: MARGIN

A topic that can often be perceived as difficult, margins must be explained thoroughly and simply. A basic approach is utilized to discuss the rules, risks, and calculations that are utilized to figure equity, SMA, and buying power, in both long and short margin accounts.

CLASS 8: TAXES AND TAX ADVANTAGE INVESTMENTS

This class briefly discusses the tax planning that a broker can assist with, as well as retirement plans and partnerships that offer unique advantages to investors in higher tax brackets.

CLASS 9: OPTIONS

A discussion of basic option contracts, as well as strategies such as combinations, straddles, spreads, and the mechanics of option trading.

The Montano Institute of Finance ("The Institute") and the people who operate it have instructed thousands of students on the NASD examination and helped them become stockbrokers. The Institute utilizes the most modern methods to convey the information to the students to prepare them for the examination.

We at Montano Securities pride ourself on our Institute of Finance and the role that it has played in preparing people to become successful stockbrokers in the United States. We are also excited about discussions that we are having with organizations in other nations about the Institute training their citizens in their nations and helping them develop their capital markets. At the Montano Institute of Finance, we are endeavoring to become one of the leading educational organizations in this new era of international commerce and Capitalism.

While passing the examination licenses a person to deal in securities, it does not make them a stockbroker in the real sense. To become a real stockbroker, a person must continue his or her education and development, establish personal relationships with clients, and seek out sources of investment products to serve the clients' needs.

The world changes too rapidly for anyone to believe that upon passing the examination, you are done learning. Stockbrokers must always remain informed of what is going on in the world around them. Information and data are the secrets to success for all stockbrokers. And we all know that life is a journey of enlightenment.

Rather than spend more time in this book on the procedures to become a stockbroker, if you wish to learn more just call 1-800-542-7424. We will send you the Montano Securities information package on "How to Become a Stockbroker." This package will provide you with more detailed information on how you can become a stockbroker.

In closing this section, I want to emphasize that the training for the examination to become a licensed stockbroker is difficult and demanding. I also tell everyone who starts on this path that they may have to take the exam more than once. I have business partners who are extremely intelligent who have had to take the examination more than once. In fact, I have one partner who previously passed the examination and was a stockbroker, a Principal, and an Officer of a securities firm. He then retired and let his license expire. When my partner returned to the business, he had to take the exam again, but this time he needed to take it twice to pass!

The primary issue to success in this business is not necessarily how smart you are, but how determined you are. I have one partner that had to take the exam 3 times, yet last year he took home $350,000. That's what counts. I want to emphasize it is determination that counts because the exam is tricky and difficult and you may have to take it more than once. However, once you are a licensed stockbroker, you are a stockbroker for life (as long as you maintain your license) and that's when the fun part starts.

The most important thing for you to remember is that to become part of the greatest business in the world, a very high paying and prestigious business, you need to work hard to become a licensed stockbroker. Once you pass, you will see that it was well worth the effort.

12

THE GREATEST BUSINESS IN THE WORLD

The stockbrokerage business is the greatest business in the world. It is dynamic, exciting, and rewarding. Throughout this book, I have been sharing with you, the reader, my vision of the future of the commercial and economic world. The basis of this book is to open the mind of the reader to the possibilities.

The world is experiencing a reawakening. The technologies of the world are creating the Communications Revolution. This Communications Revolution is opening up new possibilities. In the minds of some readers, I have left the real world with my vision of world Commercial Democracy and the resulting economic boom.

Yet, in my mind, I see a child in the middle of Africa who would have been lost to the world without the Communications Revolution. I can see that child walking outside of the mud hut that he lives in and learning all the knowledge of today's world. He simply places his laptop computer on the table, points its satellite antenna at the sky, and, through a satellite hook-up, he accesses the Smithsonian Library in Washington D.C. The computer translates the data received from English into this boy's native tongue. The computer's interactive screen allows the boy to teach himself English, math, science, and history.

This boy, who would have been otherwise lost to the outside world, can teach himself the knowledge of the world from his tiny village in the middle of Africa. From his self-taught learning, the young boy discovers a plant near his village. The boy discovers that this plant produces a chemical compound that replenishes the human kidneys. A million lives are then saved every year because of his discovery. This discovery increases life expectancy for all mankind another 3 years. Another 3 years of life for every person on the face of the earth.

Star Trek fantasy? Maybe. Maybe not.

The 21st Century is only 7 years away. In the United States, we enjoy riches and prosperity. Never in the history of the world has there existed such massive discrepancies of wealth and poverty between people on this planet. Yet, never has the world been smaller and communications more open.

How long can the wealth of knowledge and prosperity be kept away from the other 5 billion people of the world? The Elitist as Nationalist, Socialist, and Communist struggled to keep people enslaved and ignorant. They built these false dams against knowledge to restrict the flow of human genius and abilities. Those false dams of restrictions are being blown up every day by the Communications Revolution.

Free people are now using the Communications Revolution to destroy the dams built by others. At the center of all of this freedom is the new concept of Commercial Democracy, the rights of man to prosper. At the forefront of prosperity are the Capitalists, those that finance the new industries, the new businesses, and tomorrow.

The stockbrokers of the 21st Century will be different than those you see today. The stockbroker of the 21st Century will be a 78 year old retired woman in Leisure World, servicing the income and safety needs of other retirees. It will be a part-time stockbroker, driving his 16 wheeler into a truck stop, to educate 9 other truckers on how to set up a 401-K retirement plan. It will be a Filipino-American accountant in New York City showing a Filipino-American doctor how he can earn 18% on Municipal Bonds from his home, Provence in Pangasinan. It will be a Romanian-American in San Fernando Valley, California coordinating the placing of 50 million dollars worth of Romanian Power Companies Bonds.

As the dams of restrictions are blown up everywhere in the world by the Communications Revolution, the first wave of commercial life giving water will be the stockbrokers. Stockbrokers will be providing financial capital and guidance to create this economic blossoming of the world. The stockbrokers will be, as they have always been, out in front of change and innovation. It was stockbrokers who financed computers, telecommunications, medicine, bio-tech, and more. It was the stockbrokers who financed the canals and railroads in the United States in the 1700's and 1800's. The stockbrokers will not only be different in the 21st Century, they will create the 21st Century.

Yes, the 21st Century Stockbroker will be a New Wave. A New Wave that finances and promotes Commercial Democracy throughout the world. Stockbrokers will be the catalyst of the World's Economic and Financial Revolution of the 21st Century. You can become a stockbroker. You can participate and you can profit.

Can you be a stockbroker in the 21st Century? If you love life, love excitement, and have vision and passion, YES!

In closing this book, one final story. Someone once asked me, "Dan, do you really believe in this Star Trek Economy and the world's future that you speak of so passionately?" I immediately responded, "Yes." He then asked, "Do you really believe that the television program, Star Trek - The Next Generation, is a real reflection of our future?" I said, "No." If that program were attempting to be realistic, it would have a stockbroker on board the Enterprise! New frontiers and going where no man has ever gone before are not possible without a stockbroker there!

Look in the mirror. If you see someone who is ready for tomorrow, today and if that person wants to make the world a better place and make some money in the process, become a stockbroker.

Thank you for your patience in reading this book. I sincerely hope it has intrigued your mind and opened up some new thoughts. I welcome your input and comments that can improve this book or my vision of the future. In the year 2023, we will know how close I came to being correct. I pray, for the sake of the world, that it is better than what I foresee and I believe that it will be. Your Personal Creative Genius and that of 5 billion other people will exceed everything I am capable of comprehending.

The reality of tomorrow is in our meager hands. Yet, I am confident that we, all together, will make the world a better place.

My best wishes to you and your family. I pray that our paths join so that we can work together.

Thank you.